S IT,
GOOD
AT MY
E."

BEFORE
WATCHMEN

NITE OWL • DR. MANHATTAN

BEFORE
WATC

NITE OWL • DR. MANHATTAN

J. MICHAEL STRACZYNSKI
writer

ANDY KUBERT
JOE KUBERT
BILL SIENKIEWICZ
ADAM HUGHES
EDUARDO RISSO
artists

BRAD ANDERSON
LAURA MARTIN
TRISH MULVIHILL
colorists

STEVE WANDS
NICK NAPOLITANO
CLEM ROBINS
letterers

ANDY KUBERT, JOE KUBERT and **ADAM HUGHES**
with **BRAD ANDERSON** and **LAURA MARTIN**
cover artists

Watchmen created by
ALAN MOORE and **DAVE GIBBONS**

MARK CHIARELLO WILL DENNIS Editors – Original Series
CHRIS CONROY MARK DOYLE Associate Editors – Original Series
CAMILLA ZHANG Assistant Editor – Original Series
PETER HAMBOUSSI Editor
RACHEL PINNELAS Assistant Editor
ROBBIN BROSTERMAN Design Director – Books
ROBBIE BIEDERMAN Publication Design

BOB HARRAS Senior VP – Editor-in-Chief, DC Comics

DIANE NELSON President
DAN DIDIO and JIM LEE Co-Publishers
GEOFF JOHNS Chief Creative Officer
JOHN ROOD Executive VP – Sales, Marketing & Business Development
AMY GENKINS Senior VP – Business & Legal Affairs
NAIRI GARDINER Senior VP – Finance
JEFF BOISON VP – Publishing Planning
MARK CHIARELLO VP – Art Direction & Design
JOHN CUNNINGHAM VP – Marketing
TERRI CUNNINGHAM VP – Editorial Administration
ALISON GILL Senior VP – Manufacturing & Operations
HANK KANALZ Senior VP – Vertigo & Integrated Publishing
JAY KOGAN VP – Business & Legal Affairs, Publishing
JACK MAHAN VP – Business Affairs, Talent
NICK NAPOLITANO VP – Manufacturing Administration
SUE POHJA VP – Book Sales
COURTNEY SIMMONS Senior VP – Publicity
BOB WAYNE Senior VP – Sales

CHIP KIDD Cover Design

SUSTAINABLE FORESTRY INITIATIVE — Certified Chain of Custody
At Least 20% Certified Forest Content
www.sfiprogram.org
SFI-01042
APPLIES TO TEXT STOCK ONLY

LIBRARY OF CONGRESS CATALOGING-IN-PUBLICATION DATA

STRACZYNSKI, J. MICHAEL, 1954-
  BEFORE WATCHMEN : NITE OWL/DR. MANHATTAN / J. MICHAEL STRACZYNSKI, ADAM HUGHES, JOE KUBERT.
     PAGES CM. — (BEFORE WATCHMEN)
  "ORIGINALLY PUBLISHED IN SINGLE MAGAZINE FORM IN BEFORE WATCHMEN: NITE OWL 1-4, BEFORE WATCHMEN: DR. MANHATTA
1-4, BEFORE WATCHMEN: MOLOCH 1-2."
  ISBN 978-1-4012-3894-0
1. GRAPHIC NOVELS. I. HUGHES, ADAM T. II. KUBERT, JOE, 1926-2012. III. TITLE. IV. TITLE: NITE OWL/DR. MANHATTAN.
  PN6728.W386S77 2013
  741.5'973—DC23
                              2013009136

BEFORE WATCHMEN

NITE OWL

"THE HERO KNOWN TO THE PUBLIC ONLY AS NITE OWL ANNOUNCED HIS RETIREMENT TODA

--WHERE A CROWD OF ROUGHLY SEVEN THOUSAND, MANY REPRESENTING THE STUDENTS FOR A DEMOCRATIC SOCIETY, HELD AN ANTI-NUCLEAR, ANTI-DR. MANHATTAN MARCH ON WASHINGTON.

--THE PROBLEM WITH PEOPLE TODAY, YOUNG PEOPLE IN PARTICULAR, BUT THEY'RE NOT THE ONLY ONES... IS THEY ALL WANT SOMETHING FOR NOTHING.

MEANWHILE, ASTRONAUT JOHN GLENN SAYS HE'S READY TO GO FOR THE SCHEDULED LAUNCH IN FOUR DAYS OF FRIENDSHIP 7, WHICH WILL MAKE HIM AMERICA'S THIRD MAN IN SPACE AND THE FIRST TO SUCCESSFULLY ORBIT THE EARTH.

BEFORE PROHIBITION, BARS USED TO OFFER A FREE LUNCH TO GET FOLKS IN TO BUY DRINKS. BUT THERE'S NO SUCH THING AS A FREE LUNCH ANYMORE.

NO ONE'S WATCHING THE TELEVISION, WILLIAM, SHOULDN'T WE--

NOT YET. WANT TO SEE HOW THE STOCK MARKET CLOSED. BUSY DAY AT THE BANK, DIDN'T HAVE TIME TO PHONE NEW YORK.

SOMEDAY--

WHAT WAS THAT, DANNY?

--SOMEDAY THEY'LL HAVE TV'S THE SIZE OF MATCH-BOXES THAT YOU CAN CARRY IN YOUR POCKET THAT'LL GIVE YOU THE WEATHER, SPORTS, STOCK MARKET--

OF COURSE THEY WILL.

CAN I GO UPSTAIRS? I'M NOT FEELING WELL.

OF COURSE YOU CAN.

BOY LIVES TOO MUCH IN HIS HEAD, VICTORIA. TOO MUCH TIME DREAMING.

IT'S NOT GOOD FOR HIM. I HAD MY FIRST JOB BY THE TIME I WAS SEVENTEEN. MADE GOOD MONEY, TOO.

THINKS HE CAN HAVE IT EASY WHEN HE INHERITS MY MONEY. BUT THERE'S NO SUCH THING AS A FREE LUNCH.

"THAT'S IT, TAKE A GOOD LOOK AT MY FACE."

NO SUCH THING AS A FREE LUNCH

J MICHAEL STRACZYNSKI—WRITER • ANDY KUBERT—PENCILS

JOE KUBERT—INKS • BRAD ANDERSON—COLORS • NICK NAPOLITANO—LETTERS

CAMILLA ZHANG — ASST. EDITOR • MARK DOYLE — ASSOC. EDITOR • WILL DENNIS — EDITOR

ANDY KUBERT, JOE KUBERT & BRAD ANDERSON-COVER • KEVIN NOWLAN, JIM LEE WITH SCOTT WILLIAMS & ALEX SINCLAIR-VARIANT COVER

I WANT YOU TO BE ABLE TO REMEMBER IT WHEN YOU WAKE UP IN *JAIL* AND SOMEONE ASKS YOU HOW YOU GOT THERE. YOU--

UNNH!

--AND YOUR PALS.

SO. HERE'S WHAT YOU'RE GOING TO DO. I WANT YOU TO START PUTTING THESE CARS BACK TOGETHER, AND I WANT THE VIN NUMBERS OF EACH OF THEM.

AND IF YOU THINK YOU WON'T BE DECKED--I MEAN DOCKED--FOR PENMANSHIP--

THINK AGAIN.

"THANKS FOR FINDING THESE GUYS FOR US, NITE OWL."

MY PLEASURE, LIEUTENANT. BUT I NEED TO BE GOING. SUN'S UP, WHICH MEANS IT'S *LONG* PAST MY BEDTIME.

OF COURSE.

AND A HOOTY-HOOT-HOOT TO YOU, TOO.

HOOT! HOOT! HOOT! HOOT! HOOT!

THANK YOU...THANKS... JUST DOING MY JOB!

NOW IT'S TIME FOR ME TO GET BACK IN THE OWL *CAR* AND HEAD BACK TO THE OWL *CAVE* TO GET SOME OWL *SLEEP* SO I CAN COME BACK OUT AGAIN TONIGHT AND DISPENSE SOME WHAT?

OWL JUSTICE! BECAUSE JUSTICE CAN FIND YOU IN THE SHADOWS AND THE DARK!

FFFFWWW EEEEEEEEEEFFF SSSSSSHHHHH HHHHHH

...VROOOO-OOOMFWEE-EEEEE.....

COME ON, COME ON....

CHURCH BELLS...GOTTA BE ST. MARTINS ON CLIFFORD!

...BONG.... BONG.... BONG....

Four o'clock, Lincoln Park, South-east Corner, Green Bench.

--AND THEY *SAID* YOU COULD GET THE FABRIC IN A DR. MANHATTAN PRINT THAT ADJUSTS TO YOUR BODY TEMPERATURE, BUT APPARENTLY THERE WAS A PROBLEM IN THE MANUFACTURING--

SO. LET ME TELL YOU HOW EASY IT WAS TO *FIND* YOU AND HOW YOU CAN KEEP SOMEONE ELSE FROM DOING IT. MR. MASON.

--AND I'VE WORKED ON SOME PRETTY GREAT ELECTRONICS THAT COULD BE USEFUL, I HAVE AN IDEA FOR A FLYING VEHICLE, NIGHT-VISION GLASSES--

THE POINT BEING WHAT?

I WANT TO WORK WITH YOU, LIKE A *SIDEKICK* OR--

I'LL... THINK ABOUT IT.

YOU'RE A GO-GETTER, AND YOU HAVE SOME GREAT IDEAS, BUT I USUALLY WORK ALONE. STILL--

--I'LL BE IN TOUCH. YOU'RE A GOOD KID. I THINK YOU'VE GOT POTENTIAL.

BUT DON'T *EVER* DO AGAIN WHAT YOU DID TODAY. IF I HADN'T SEEN YOU COMING IN TIME TO REALIZE YOU WERE STILL JUST A KID--

--THIS COULD HAVE GONE VERY, VERY *BADLY* FOR YOU.

BEG FOR IT--

STOP IT, PLEASE--

--LOUDER!

-- I MEAN IT, LEAVE ME ALONE!

WHAT ARE YOU LOOKING AT! GET UPSTAIRS!

MOM--

NO... IT'S...IT'S OKAY, HONE YOU GO UP. PLEASE....

...PLEASE....

IF WE COULD JUST...DO THIS LATER, WILLIAM, I--

HELL WITH HIM. ABOUT TIME HE SAW HOW A *MAN* BEHAVES. MAYBE HE'LL LEARN A FEW THINGS.

STARTED THAT PROCESS ALREADY...TIME HE GREW UP A LITTLE...STOPPED PLAYING WITH GODDAMN *DOLLS*.

YOU SHOULD GO INSIDE. IT'S COLD.

OH, AND AT SOME POINT YOU SHOULD CALL THE HOSPITAL.

LOOKS LIKE YOUR FATHER'S HAD A HEART ATTACK.

I'D DO IT MYSELF, BUT FOR SOME REASON I JUST CAN'T REMEMBER THE PHONE NUMBER.

I SAW THE BRUISES. READ THE POLICE REPORTS. SO I WON'T SAY I'M **SORRY** FOR YOUR LOSS.

YEAH.

SO I... GUESS WE SHOULD GET STARTED.

YEAH, I GUESS SO.

"--BUT IT'LL ALL WORK OUT IN THE END, YOU'LL SEE."

-- AS THE COUNTRY WAS ROCKED TODAY WITH UNEXPECTED NEWS FROM THE WORLD OF CRIME FIGHTERS.

IN A PREPARED STATEMENT GIVEN TO KNOWN ASSOCIATES AND CONTACTS IN THE FBI, THE HERO KNOWN TO THE PUBLIC ONLY AS NITE OWL ANNOUNCED HIS *RETIREMENT*.

WHEN ASKED ABOUT FUTURE PLANS, THE HERO SOME CALL *"THE LIGHT IN THE DARKNESS"* SAID ONLY THAT HE WAS GOING TO TAKE SOME TIME TO RELAX, TEACH, AND POSSIBLY WRITE A BOOK.

SO WHEN WERE YOU PLANNING TO TELL ME?

AND WHY DID I HAVE TO FIND OUT YOU WERE RETIRING ON THE *NEWS*?

WASN'T SURE MYSELF UNTIL TODAY. I'VE THOUGHT ABOUT IT ON AND OFF FOR A WHILE NOW. NEVER HAD THE COURAGE TO GO THROUGH WITH IT, UNTIL NOW.

YEAH? AND WHAT'S DIFFERENT *NOW*?

THERE'S YOU.

YOU'RE HERE TO PICK UP WHERE I LEFT OFF...SO THE NAME NITE OWL DOESN'T JUST UP AND DISAPPEAR. CALL IT PRIDE, I GUESS, BUT THAT WAS THE ONLY THING STILL KEEPING ME GOING.

THERE'S THINGS YOU DON'T KNOW ABOUT ME, DANIEL...THINGS I DIDN'T EVEN KNOW ABOUT **MYSELF** UNTIL--

--UNTIL RECENTLY.

TERRIBLE....

THERE ARE THINGS YOU LEARN ABOUT YOURSELF, ABOUT THE PERSON YOU REALLY ARE, AS OPPOSED TO THE PERSON YOU **THINK** YOU ARE, THAT MAKE YOU ASK THE ONE QUESTION NOBODY WANTS TO ASK.

WHY AM I STILL DOING WHAT I'VE BEEN DOING MY WHOLE LIFE?

WHATEVER IT IS YOU'VE BEEN **DOING**, WHATEVER IT MAY HAVE **MEANT** TO YOU, THE DAY YOU ASK THAT QUESTION IS THE DAY YOU HAVE TO STOP DOING IT. BECAUSE IT DOESN'T MEAN WHAT IT **USED** TO ANYMORE.

SO I'M GIVING IT ALL TO YOU, DANIEL. THE NAME, THE REP, THE GADGETS--

--THOUGH I THINK YOU'LL OUTCLASS ME ON THAT SCORE PRETTY FAST--

--NO OWLIE, NO OWL-BOY, NO OWL-KID, JUST LIKE I PROMISED.

FROM NOW ON, **YOU'RE** THE NITE OWL.

WE JUST HAVE TO FINISH TRAINING YOU.

AND... UHM...HOW LONG DO YOU THINK THAT'LL TAKE?

WELL, YOU GOTTA FINISH COLLEGE TO SMARTEN YOU UP, GET IN PRIME FIGHTING SHAPE, BUILD UP YOUR WEIGHT, TRY SOME TEST JOBS WITHOUT THE NITE OWL GEAR, BUILD THAT OWL SHIP OF YOURS--

ARCHIMEDES...I'VE DECIDED TO CHRISTEN IT ARCHIMEDES--

SWELL.

ALL IN...MAYBE TWO, THREE YEARS....

"THEN, SUDDENLY, EVERYTHING WENT **DARK**."

ARCHIMEDES... CLOUD.

DON'T LIKE IT. COULD BE A TRAP.

THE INVITATION CAME FROM CAPTAIN METROPOLIS PERSONALLY.

EVER MET HIM BEFORE?

THEN COULD BE A TRAP.

NO, BUT--

EXCUSE ME--

IS THIS WHERE THE BIG MEETING IS TAKING PLACE?

I-- --I MEAN, YES...

YES, IT IS. YOU'RE THE SILK SPECTRE, RIGHT?

HURM.

YES.

NITE OWL AND RORSCHACH.

HURM.

GOOD TO MEET YOU. WELL, I GUESS I'LL SEE YOU INSIDE.

SUIT TIGHT AS YOURS MUST BE UNCOMFORTABLE RIGHT NOW.

HEY, WATCH IT, I-- --WELL, YES, BUT--

--I JUST HAD THIS FEELING, WHEN I SAW HER...I GOT CHILLS.

PROBABLY SAME FEELING AS WHEN PEOPLE SAY SOMEONE JUST WALKED OVER THEIR GRAVE.

HURM.

"I GUESS I SHOULD WELCOME EVERYBODY TO THE FIRST EVER MEETING OF THE CRIMEBUSTERS."

IF CRIMEBUSTERS IS TO BECOME AN EFFICIENT CRIME FIGHTING ORGANIZATION, IT'S IMPORTANT THAT WE LEARN TO WORK TOGETHER.

BURP!

I'D LIKE TO START BY PAIRING PEOPLE UP INTO GROUPS OF TWO, SO WE CAN LEARN ABOUT EACH OTHER'S IDEAS, GOALS, AND WHAT WE HOPE TO ACHIEVE WITH CRIMEBUSTERS. THAT'S WHY I HAD EACH OF YOU PUT YOUR I.D. ON A SLIP OF PAPER.

STATES OF

OUR FIRST IS DR. MANHATTAN, WHOSE PRESENCE HERE TONIGHT HONORS ALL OF US--

--AND THE ONE HE'S PARTNERED WITH TONIGHT IS--

--IS--

--THE SILK SPECTRE. NEXT IS--

WHY CRIME-BUSTERS?

Silk Spectre

WHY "THE CRIMEBUSTERS"?

WELL, AS YOU KNOW, THIS COUNTRY HASN'T HAD AN ORGANIZATION OF *MASKED ADVENTURERS* SINCE THE *MINUTEMEN* DISBANDED IN '49.

...PECIALIZED LAW ENFORCEMENT IS *STANDING STILL.* CRIME *ISN'T.* NEW SOCIAL EVILS EMERGE EVERY DAY--

--*PROMISCUITY, DRUGS, CAMPUS SUBVERSION,* YOU *NAME* IT! NOW, BY BANDING TOGETHER AS THE CRIMEBUSTERS, WE--

BULLSHIT.

"BULLSHIT, HE SAID."

I DIDN'T THINK HEROES WERE SUPPOSED TO TALK LIKE THAT. AND THEN THAT WHOLE BUSINESS OF BURNING THE MAP--

FIRST TIME SEEING THE COMEDIAN?

YES.

LUCKY HE DIDN'T BURN DOWN THE BUILDING. WITH US IN IT.

I SAID I WANT TO GO HOME RIGHT NOW.

I DON'T KNOW--

DON'T KNOW WHAT?

I JUST FELT THE STRANGEST SENSE OF CONNECTION TO HER. WHEN CAPTAIN METROPOLIS STARTED PAIRING PEOPLE UP, I WAS SURE IT WOULD BE ME AND HER, LIKE WE WERE FATED TO BE TOGETHER--

DISAPPOINTED.

YES.

WOMEN. HE SAVED YOU TROUBLE.

MAYBE.

LISTEN, HOW ABOUT WE GET SOME LUNCH?

NEARLY MIDNIGHT.

WE WORK THE NIGHT SHIFT, SO THIS IS LUNCH. MY TREAT.

WELL.

WHO CAN SAY NO TO A FREE LUNCH?

HURM.

NITE OWL

NITE OWL

"THEY RUN...I LIKE IT WHEN THEY RUN."

THEY RUN.

I *LIKE* IT WHEN THEY RUN.

HUNH...HUNH... WHERE'D THEY GO? DID YOU SEE WHICH WAY THEY--

BUT NOT AS MUCH AS *HE* DOES.

SOME THINGS ARE JUST INEVITABLE

J MICHAEL STRACZYNSKI—WRITER • ANDY KUBERT—PENCILS

JOE KUBERT—INKS • BRAD ANDERSON—COLORS • NICK NAPOLITANO—LETTERS

CAMILLA ZHANG — ASST. EDITOR • MARK DOYLE — ASSOC. EDITOR • WILL DENNIS — EDITOR

ANDY KUBERT, JOE KUBERT & BRAD ANDERSON—COVER • DAVID FINCH & SONIA OBACK—VARIANT COVER

GOOD THING I WAS IN HERE CHECKING ON MY GIRLS OR THIS COULD'VE GONE BADLY.

OH...SO YOU WEREN'T--

NO, BUT I STILL LIKE TO-- --SUPERVISE.

MMMPH....

IT'S JUST...FROM THE WAY YOU'RE--

NAKED?

I...YES... I MEAN...NO OFFENSE, BUT--

YOU'RE BLUSHING UNDER THAT MASK, AREN'T YOU?

NO, OF COURSE NOT--

MMPH?

SILENCE, WORM!

MMMPH MMMPH-MMPH...

I LIKE THE FEEL OF THE NIGHT AIR. SAME AS YOU.

I DIDN'T SAY I LIKED IT.

YOU DIDN'T HAVE TO.

CAUGHT THE OTHER ONE.

I --

SLUT.

WHORE!

YOU SAY THAT LIKE IT WAS A *BAD* THING.

RORSCHACH, NO!

BACK OFF--

ONLY ONE WAY TO--

--DAMN IT, SHE HELPED US!

DON'T CARE.

I SAID *BACK OFF!*

SMACK

MMMMPH!

I'M SORRY I HAD TO DO THAT, BUT--

NEVER APOLOGIZE. MAKES YOU WEAK.

LEAVE YOU AND THE SLUT. DO WHAT YOU WANT.

LOOK... C'MON, DON'T BE LIKE THAT.

NICE HORSE. EXPECT TO SEE YOU ON IT SOON.

I HAVE TO GO...HE'S MY PARTNER AND--

WHAT ABOUT YOUR TOY?

WHO?

THE MAN YOU WERE CHASING.

RIGHT...

THANKS ξUNHξ FOR THE HELP--

NO PROBLEM. COME AGAIN SOON.

I DIDN'T GET YOUR NAME.

THEN I GUESS YOU'LL JUST HAVE TO COME BACK FOR IT.

RORSCHACH?

RORSCHACH?

FINE... WHATEVER... SEE YOU AT THE OWL CAVE.

THERE ARE DAYS I DON'T KNOW WHAT THE HELL TO MAKE OF RORSCHACH.

WE ALL DO THE SECRET IDENTITY THING, BUT FOR MOST OF US IT'S JUST A MATTER OF HAVING ANOTHER NAME TO HIDE BEHIND.

WITH RORSCHACH, IT'S LIKE THERE ARE TWO DIFFERENT PEOPLE BEHIND THAT MASK, FIGHTING IT OUT.

AND I WONDER SOMETIMES WHAT'LL HAPPEN WHEN ONE OF THEM WINS? AND WHAT IF IT'S THE *WRONG* ONE?

--WHERE RICHARD SPECK WAS ARRESTED YESTERDAY ON CHARGES OF MURDERING EIGHT STUDENT NURSES IN THEIR CHICAGO DORMITORY--

CLICK!

--RACE RIOTS IN CLEVELAND CONTINUED TO SPIRAL OUT OF CONTROL AS COLORED PROTESTERS BATTLED POLICE FROM SEVERAL--

CLICK!

--GEMINI 10 DOCKED WITH THE AGENA TARGET VESSEL--

THE NEW *PLAYTEX* LIVING BRA, IT LIFTS AND SEPARATES FOR A CLEANER, MORE NATURAL APPEARANCE.

IT *LIFTS* AND *SEPARATES*.

IT LIFTS.

AND SEPARATES.

CROSS YOUR HEART.

WHUD-WHUD-WHUD-WHUD

FOR A CLEANER, MORE NATURAL APPEARANCE.

"BE CAREFUL, DAN. YOU CAN'T TRUST HER."

SO YOU KNOW HER?

ME AND EVERY VICE COP IN THE CITY. CALLS HERSELF THE *TWILIGHT LADY*. RUNS A STABLE OF HIGH-PRICED CALL GIRLS AND FETISH OPERATIONS.

SHE'S TROUBLE.

WHAT KIND OF TROUBLE?

THE KIND YOU WANT NO PART OF. EVEN IF YOU BUST ANY OF HER OPERATIONS, JUST BEING IN THE SAME PHOTO AS HER OR ANY OF HER CLIENTS CAN TAINT THE NITE OWL NAME. MAKES YOU LESS KID-FRIENDLY AS A HERO.

YOU WANT MY ADVICE? STICK WITH BUSTING CON ARTISTS, STICK-UPS AND BANK ROBBERIES. CLEANER THAT WAY.

PEOPLE NEED A HERO THEY CAN *BELIEVE* IN. YOU CAN'T LET YOURSELF DO ANYTHING THAT MIGHT DESTROY THAT, ANYTHING THAT MIGHT --

"--THAT MIGHT--"

--MAKE YOU REALIZE THAT AN AWFUL LOT OF YOUR LIFE WAS JUST A LIE.

COME ON, RORSCHACH...

...WHERE *ARE* YOU? STILL MAD ABOUT LAST NIGHT? STILL SULKING IN WHATEVER HOLE-IN-THE-WALL YOU CALL HOME?

FINE. SUIT YOURSELF.

THE **HONORABLE MAN** IN **DISHONORABLE TIMES.**

"OUR PROBLEM TODAY IS A MATTER OF *NOISE.* OUR PROBLEM TODAY IS A MATTER OF *VOLUME.*"

TELEVISION IS LOUD. MOVIES ARE LOUD. AND THE MUSIC THESE YOUNG PEOPLE LISTEN TO TODAY IS LOUD AS HELL BECAUSE THAT'S WHERE IT COMES FROM.

PEOPLE COME TO ME EVERY DAY, GOOD PEOPLE, AND THEY SAY, "PASTOR DEAN, HOW DO WE COMPETE WITH THAT? THE SINS OF THE WORLD ARE DROWNING US OUT."

WELL, I CAN TELL YOU WHAT WE *DON'T* DO. WE DON'T GET *QUIET*, WE DON'T SURRENDER THE *BATTLEFIELD*, WE DON'T ABANDON *SHIP*, WE DON'T ALLOW OURSELVES TO BE *SILENCED*.

SO WHAT DO WE DO?

WE GET LOUDER!

ONE MORE TIME!

WE GET LOUDER!

GET LOUDER.

BECAUSE WE HAVE TO SEND THE MESSAGE THAT WE ARE RUNNING OUT OF *TIME*. IT'S A MESSAGE PEOPLE HAVE TO HEAR, BY ANY AND ALL MEANS NECESSARY.

THE END IS NIGH

GET LOUD. IT'S THE ONLY WAY WE WILL *EVER* MAKE THE WORLD *LISTEN* TO US.

9-ADAM-4, HOMICIDE REPORT, 327 GRANT STREET, SEE THE MANAGER.

COPY, DISPATCH, ON OUR WAY.

"SO WHAT HAVE WE GOT?"

NAME WAS SALLY ROSE, AT LEAST THAT'S THE NAME SHE RENTED THE PLACE UNDER.

THE NEIGHBOR SAYS SHE WAS A HOOKER.

I DON'T KNOW NOTHIN' ABOUT THAT, I JUST RENT THE PLACE OUT.

WAS SHE WITH A CLIENT?

THOUGHT THIS SORT OF THING WASN'T YOUR SORT OF THING, NITE OWL.

MAYBE I SHOULD DECIDE THAT FOR MYSELF.

SO LIKE I SAID, WAS SHE WITH A CLIENT?

AND LIKE I SAID, I DON'T KNOW NOTHIN'--

I NOTICED A SECURITY CAMERA IN THE HALL.

DOESN'T WORK.

ON EVERY FLOOR OR JUST THIS FLOOR?

THIS ONE.

NICE LITTLE COINCIDENCE, ISN'T IT?

SO *NO ONE* SAW ANYTHING?

NO.

AND YOU KNOW THAT *HOW?*

NO ONE SEES. EVER.

KITTY GENOVESE. NEW YORK. MARCH 13, 1964. 3:15 A.M. STABBED, ATTACKED FOR OVER HALF AN HOUR IN HER APARTMENT LOBBY.

THIRTY-EIGHT NEIGHBORS HEARD WHOLE THING.

NO ONE CALLED POLICE.

NO ONE HELPED.

NO ONE HEARD.

NO ONE SAW.

NO ONE CARED.

WHORES DIE EVERY DAY. NO ONE SEES. THIS ISN'T THE FIRST.

IS THIS THE FIRST? OR HAVE THERE BEEN *MORE?*

DON'T MAKE ME ASK A SECOND TIME.

ONE MORE DEAD SLUT.

IT DOESN'T MATTER.

WONDERED IF I WAS GOING TO SEE YOU AGAIN.

LOST MY HEAD.

ME TOO.

PERSONAL SITUATION.

ME TOO.

FUNNY WORLD. FULL OF SURPRISES.

YEAH. DID YOU WANT TO TALK ABOUT--

NO. YOU?

NO.

GOOD.

ONE THING... SEEMS TO ME YOU KNOW A LOT ABOUT THE KITTY GENOVESE MURDER. ANY REASON IN PARTICULAR?

NIGHT I HEARD THE NEWS... NIGHT I HEARD 38 PEOPLE DID NOTHING... WAS THE NIGHT I PUT ON THIS MASK. NEVER WANTED TO SEE FACE IN MIRROR AGAIN.

ASHAMED TO BE PART OF HUMAN RACE.

SO I'M NOT. NOT ANY-MORE.

ENOUGH TALK.

LET'S GO HIT SOMETHING.

NO SON OF MINE IS GOING TO GET BEAT UP IN A FIGHT, HE SAYS. SO WE JUST WON'T LET HIM SEE IT, THAT'S ALL.

OWCH! BOY, IT HURTS--

YOU JUST HAVE TO LEARN TO MAKE IT SMALL, DANNY, SO IT CAN'T HURT YOU.

HOW? HOW DO--

--HOW DO YOU DO IT?

YOU HAVE TO FIND A PLACE DEEP INSIDE WHERE NOBODY CAN TOUCH YOU OR HURT YOU. IT CAN BE SOMETHING YOU REMEMBER, SOMETHING HAPPY--

--SOMETHING THAT MAKES YOU ANGRY--

--BUT IT HAS TO BE SOMETHING SPECIAL TO YOU--

"--THAT YOU CAN PUT BETWEEN YOURSELF AND THE *DRAGON*."

WHERE NITE OWL ONCE AGAIN TRIUMPHED.

WE CAPTURED THESE IMAGES OF THE TERROR OF THE NIGHT IN ACTION AGAINST SUPERIOR NUMBERS.

DESPITE THE OVERWHELMING ODDS, DESPITE BEING KNOCKED DOWN AGAIN AND AGAIN, THE NITE OWL KEEPS GETTING UP...WOUNDED AND BLEEDING, HE KEEPS FIGHTING...

NOTHING STOPS HIM, NOT PAIN, NOT BLOOD, NOT BROKEN BONES...HE GETS UP...AND HE KEEPS FIGHTING...HE KEEPS FIGHTING...

HEY...GUYS... CHECK IT.

LET'S GO.

WHERE YOU GOIN'?

JERK DOESN'T KNOW WHEN HE'S BEAT.

NOT BEAT. I DIDN'T GIVE.

I KNOW I CAN'T WIN...BUT AS LONG AS I DON'T GIVE...

...YOU CAN'T WIN EITHER.

HEY...GUYS... CHECK IT.

COME ON...

...YOU CAN'T *HURT* ME... YOU CAN'T *TOUCH* ME...

...LET'S GO.

"SO WHICH OF YOU WANTED ME?"

WHAT DO YOU MEAN?

I HEARD YOU AND DAD TALKING THE OTHER DAY, AND--

--HE SAID THE ONLY REASON YOU GOT MARRIED WAS BECAUSE YOU WERE PREGNANT WITH ME, AND THERE WAS A--

--A DISAGREEMENT OVER WHAT TO DO ABOUT IT.

BUT I'M HERE... SO THAT MEANS EITHER YOU WANTED ME AND HE DIDN'T, AND HE WAS FORCED TO GET MARRIED--

--OR HE WANTED ME, BECAUSE HE WANTED A SON, AND YOU DIDN'T.

SO... WHO WAS IT WHO WANTED ME?

IT DOESN'T MATTER ANYMORE, DANNY.

IT DOESN'T MATTER.

DOESN'T MATTER.

"ONE MORE DEAD SLUT."

"DOESN'T MATTER."

NO. IT **DOES** MATTER.

IT **HAS TO** MATTER.

I KNEW YOU'D BE BACK.

NITE OWL

"A MAN LIKE YOU LOVES A MYSTERY."

THANKS FOR COMING

J MICHAEL STRACZYNSKI–WRITER • **ANDY KUBERT**–PENCILS

JOE KUBERT & BILL SIENKIEWICZ–INKS • **BRAD ANDERSON**–COLORS • **NICK NAPOLITANO**–LETTERS
CAMILLA ZHANG – ASST. EDITOR • **MARK DOYLE** – ASSOC. EDITOR • **WILL DENNIS** – EDITOR
ANDY KUBERT, JOE KUBERT & BRAD ANDERSON–COVER • **CHRIS SAMNEE & MATT WILSON**–VARIANT COVER

I DID SOME DIGGING AND CONFIRMED THAT SEVERAL OTHER CALL GIRLS HAVE BEEN MURDERED IN THE LAST MONTH.

AND A LOT MORE HAVE GONE *MISSING*. BUT SO FAR THE POLICE HAVE BEEN --

--UNINTERESTED?

SOMETHING LIKE THAT.

SO IF YOU *KNOW* SOMETHING --

I DON'T KNOW ANY MORE THAN YOU DO. BUT I HAVE MY SUSPICIONS.

THEN TELL ME WHAT THEY--

NO. BETTER IF I *SHOW* YOU.

YOU'RE GOING WITH ME?

IF I WERE *GOING* WITH YOU WE'D BE *DATING*. SO INSTEAD I'LL JUST --

--COME WITH YOU.

I--

WAIT... WHERE ARE YOU--

IF WE'RE GOING TO BE RUNNING AROUND ON ROOFTOPS, I WANT TO CHANGE INTO SOMETHING MORE COMFORTABLE.

MORE COMFORTABLE...?

"...WHERE AFTER FOUR DAYS FIRES ARE STILL RAGING OUT OF CONTROL-

CLICK

--AS RACE RIOTS CONTINUE IN CLEVELAND. THREE WHITE MEN WERE ARRESTED TODAY FOR SHOOTING BENORIS TONEY, A 29-YEAR-OLD BLACK MAN. THE MEN CLAIM THEY ACTED IN SELF-DEFENSE BUT OTHER WITNESSES--

ALWAYS THE FIRST TO SHOW UP FOR WORK AND THE LAST TO LEAVE. YOU'RE MAKING ME LOOK BAD BY COMPARISON, WALTER.

SORRY, REVEREND DEAN.

EVERY TIME I SEE YOU, YOU'VE GOT THE NEWS ON. WHY IS THAT?

NEWS IS HOW THE WORLD CRIES OUT IN PAIN. **NEED** TO HEAR IT. CONSTANTLY. OVER AND OVER.

SO YOU CAN FEEL THEIR **PAIN?**

SO I **CAN'T.** MAKES ME NUMB.

IF I CAN'T FEEL MY HANDS, THEY CAN DO WHAT I NEED THEM TO DO.

I SWEAR, SOME DAYS YOU DON'T SAY A WORD AND OTHER DAYS YOU TALK LIKE THAT WRITER, GINSBERG.

"I SAW THE BEST MINDS OF MY GENERATION DESTROYED BY MADNESS, STARVING HYSTERICAL NAKED, DRAGGING THEMSELVES THROUGH THE NEGRO STREETS AT DAWN LOOKING FOR AN ANGRY FIX."

HE WAS A COMMUNIST, YOU KNOW. ALSO QUEER AS A THREE DOLLAR BILL.

THE NEWS YOU WERE LISTENING TO OUT OF CLEVELAND...IN THREE YEARS WE'VE HAD RACE RIOTS IN HARLEM, ROCHESTER, PHILADELPHIA, WATTS, CHICAGO...AND NOW THIS.

BUT THE REAL PROBLEM ISN'T RACE, WALTER. BLACK, WHITE, BROWN, ASIAN, WE'RE ALL GOD'S CHILDREN.

THE PROBLEM IS IMMORALITY AND SPIRITUAL DECAY. SEX AND DRUGS AND PERMISSIVENESS.

"IF THINGS CONTINUE AS THEY ARE, IF NOBODY STOPS IT, WE'RE GOING TO HAVE MORE RIOTS, MORE DEATH, MORE PAIN --

--UNTIL THE WHOLE WORLD IS JUST ONE GREAT BIG SMOKING CINDER."

OF ALL MY FLOCK, I THINK YOU MAY BE ONE OF THE FEW WHO REALLY UNDERSTANDS WHAT I'M SAYING, WALTER. DO YOU?

YES, REVEREND.

THEN VERY SOON I MAY HAVE A TASK FOR YOU.

A CHANCE TO STRIKE A BLOW FOR ALL THAT IS RIGHT AND DECENT. WOULD YOU LIKE THAT?

YES, REVEREND.

THEN I'LL LET YOU FINISH YOUR WORK. GOOD NIGHT, WALTER.

GOOD NIGHT, REVEREND.

FUNNY THING, THOUGH.

WHAT'S THAT?

GINSBERG. YOU SAID COMMUNIST. QUEER AS A THREE-DOLLAR BILL. BUT YOU STILL REMEMBER THE POEM.

GOOD NIGHT, WALTER.

--AS PRE-TRIAL MOTIONS BEGAN TODAY IN THE CASE OF RICHARD SPECK.

SPECK, TWENTY-FOUR, IS ACCUSED OF RAPING, TORTURING AND MURDERING EIGHT STUDENT NURSES FROM SOUTH CHICAGO COMMUNITY HOSPITAL.

WE'LL HAVE MORE NEWS AFTER THIS BRIEF WORD FROM OUR SPONSOR.

ANYTIME, ANYWHERE, BAD BREATH CAN PUT YOU IN ISOLATION. SUDDENLY YOU'LL FEEL LEFT OUT, SET APART. THAT'S THE TIME FOR CLORETS.

YES... NUMB... CAN'T FEEL A THING.

THE END IS NI[GH]

I SAW THE BEST MINDS OF MY GENERATION DESTROYED BY MADNESS.

THAT'S THE TIME FOR CLORETS.

THE END IS NIGH

IT'S JUST A LITTLE FARTHER--

UH-HUH--

--AND I'LL NEED YOU TO PAY ATTENTION TO WHAT I SHOW YOU, NOT MY **ASS**.

I WASN'T LOOKING AT YOUR --

SHHH....

THAT'S CARLOS ONOFRIO, A COLOMBIAN WHO'S SET UP A PROSTITUTION RING ON THE SOUTH SIDE OF THE CITY.

HE'S THE ONE YOU NEED TO QUESTION.

HOW DO I KNOW YOU'RE NOT JUST USING ME TO TAKE OUT THE COMPETITION?

COMPETITION? HARDLY.

MY GIRLS ARE **PROS**, HIGH-CLASS ESCORTS.

CARLOS RECRUITS RIGHT OFF THE BOAT OR THE BUS DEPOT: POLES, CZECHS, RUSSIANS AND SOUTH AMERICANS.

GETS THEM HOOKED ON DRUGS THEN PUTS THEM TO WORK ON THE LOWER TRACK, DOWNTOWN STREETS AND THE DOCKS.

"ONE OF HIS GIRLS GOT AWAY, CAME TO ME FOR HELP. SHE TOLD ME THAT THREE OF THE GIRLS WHO CAME WITH HER FROM THE UKRAINE HAD DISAPPEARED. SHE COULDN'T PROVE IT BUT SHE WAS PRETTY SURE THEY'D BEEN KILLED, EITHER BY CARLOS OR SOMEONE CLOSE TO HIM."

WHY DIDN'T SHE GO TO THE POLICE?

LET'S SEE...ILLEGAL IMMIGRANT, DRUGS IN HER SYSTEM, WORKING AS A HOOKER...YEAH, THE COPS ARE THE FIRST PLACE **I'D** THINK OF GOING.

AND EVEN IF THEY BELIEVED HER, SO WHAT? AS YOUR FRIEND MIGHT SAY, WHAT'S ONE MORE DEAD **WHORE**?

IF THEY'RE NOT YOUR GIRLS, WHY DO YOU CARE? NO SKIN OFF YOUR NOSE.

I COME TO WHERE I AM BY A HARD ROAD. LOTS OF OTHER GIRLS ON THAT ROAD FELL DOWN AND NEVER GOT UP AGAIN.

I WAS ALMOST ONE OF THEM. SO I SWORE I'D CREATE AN ENVIRONMENT WHERE GIRLS WHO MADE THE SAME MISTAKES I MADE COULD AT LEAST BE SAFE.

UH-HUH. SO YOU DON'T *EXPLOIT* THEM.

NO, DARLING...IT'S MEN LIKE *YOU* I EXPLOIT.

SO YOU THINK I CAN BE EXPLOITED?

MAYBE *TRUSTED* IS A BETTER WORD. I KNEW I COULD TRUST YOU THE MOMENT I SAW YOUR EYES.

I'M WEARING GOGGLES.

MMMM... MEN ARE SO NAIVE.

LET ME KNOW WHAT YOU FIND.

I DIDN'T SAY I WAS GOING TO QUESTION HIM.

SO VERY, VERY NAIVE.

...CRAP.

--THE OO7 COLLECTION: AFTER-SHAVE, HAIRDRESSING...

...FOR THE LICENSE TO KILL... WOMEN.

CLICK
CLICK
CLICK

SONOFABITCH... DEAD BULB--

HELLO, CARLOS.

CLICK

UNNHH!

I HEAR YOU'VE BEEN CARELESS WITH SOME OF YOUR WOMEN, CARLOS. I'VE LOST KEYS, SPARE CHANGE --

--MY MIND--

--BUT NEVER AN ENTIRE WOMAN. SO WHAT HAPPENED TO THEM?

AAGGHH--

I'M NOT GOING TO ASK YOU AGAIN!

WELL, NO, ACTUALLY I AM GOING TO ASK YOU AGAIN BECAUSE I DON'T WANT YOU TO THINK I'VE LOST INTEREST IN THE ANSWER, SO--

--WOMEN. MISSING. DEAD. HOW? WHERE? WHY? AND MAINLY--

--WHO?

CRASH

NOW YOU'RE IN TROUBLE, ASSHOLE.

FUNNY, I WAS ABOUT TO SAY THE SAME THING TO YOU.

WELL, IN THE PLURAL FORM.

"DID YOU KNOW THAT EVERY YEAR, 1.2 MILLION PEOPLE DIE BY DROWNING?"

DID YOU KNOW THEY ALSO SAY THAT HUNDREDS OF PEOPLE DIE EACH YEAR IN LESS THAN SIX INCHES OF WATER?

--NO--

--NO--

I'VE ALWAYS FOUND IT HARD TO BELIEVE THAT'S POSSIBLE. DO YOU FIND IT HARD TO BELIEVE, CARLOS?

--NO--

SO I GUESS YOU DON'T WANT TO HELP ME WITH MY LITTLE EXPERIMENT, FIND OUT WHETHER OR NOT THAT'S REALLY TRUE.

GOD NO.

THEN TELL ME WHAT I WANT TO KNOW.

WHEN THE GIRLS ARE NEW EVERYBODY WANTS 'EM, WE PUT 'EM UP SOMEWHERE NICE, GET TOP DOLLAR, SIX, SEVEN HUNDRED BUCKS A THROW.

WHEN THEY GET WORN DOWN THEY MOVE TO THE NEXT LEVEL, TWO, MAYBE THREE HUNDRED.

AFTER THAT, IT'S THE STREETS. AND AFTER THE STREETS--

THERE'S GUYS WHO BUY OLD CARS, SELL 'EM FOR PARTS.

GUYS WHO BUY WASHING MACHINES, TVS, STUFF THAT GETS THROWN AWAY... AND GUYS WHO BUY *LEFTOVERS* FROM PEOPLE LIKE ME.

WHAT THEY DO WITH 'EM...I DON'T ASK.

I WANT NAMES AND NUMBERS.

I DON'T GOT NAMES, JUST NUMBERS.

THEN GIVE THEM TO ME. ALL OF THEM.

RIGHT.

NOW!

"HE MADE YOU ANGRY, DIDN'T HE?"

YES. BUT I GOT WHAT I NEEDED. SIX PHONE NUMBERS. I'LL RUN THEM DOWN, SEE WHAT I CAN FIND. I--

AND YOU WANTED TO *HURT* HIM, DIDN'T YOU?

-- YES.

I'VE FOUND THAT MEN EITHER LOVE AND DEFEND WOMEN WHO REMIND THEM OF THEIR MOTHERS OR ATTACK AND HATE WOMEN WHO REMIND THEM OF THEIR MOTHERS. I FEEL SOME CONFLICT IN YOU.

DID SHE PROTECT YOU? OR LEAVE YOU TO THE WOLVES?

MY MOTHER WASN'T A--

I DIDN'T SAY SHE WAS. BUT SHE WAS USED AND ABUSED, WASN'T SHE?

I...HOW DID WE END UP IN YOUR BEDROOM?

MEN USE MONEY OR FORCE TO TRY AND MAKE US SERVE THEM, TURN US INTO WHORES. WHEN IT WORKS, SOME OF US TURN THE LIGHTS OFF, SO WE DON'T HAVE TO THINK ABOUT WHAT WE'RE DOING.

SOME LEAVE THE LIGHTS ON BECAUSE WE *WANT* A FACE TO GO WITH OUR RAGE. AND SOME FIGHT TO TURN IT AROUND FOR OUR OWN BENEFIT.

SO WHICH ARE YOU?

I WORKED MY WAY THROUGH ALL THREE.

NO. THIS IS SO NOT GOING TO WORK.

WHY NOT?

THIS DOESN'T STRIKE YOU AS A BIT... ODD?

I THOUGHT YOU SPECIALIZED IN ODD.

I DO.

BUT THERE'S ODD, AND THERE'S ODD, AND THIS IS ODD.

I CAN'T TAKE OFF MY MASK --

YES YOU CAN. LOOK, I'LL TELL YOU WHAT.

AS LONG AS YOU'RE NOT ANYONE FAMOUS, THE ODDS OF EITHER OF US RECOGNIZING THE OTHER ARE PRETTY MUCH ZERO. SO I'LL GO FIRST TO PROVE THE POINT.

THERE... DO YOU HAVE ANY IDEA WHO I AM?

NO. NONE.

OKAY, SEE? I DID IT AND IT'S FINE. SO NOW IT'S YOUR TURN.

I--

--WELL, I SUPPOSE YOU'RE RIGHT, THE ODDS ARE ABOUT ONE IN TEN MILLION, AND IT IS PRETTY DARK IN HERE.

THERE. SO NOW I GUESS WE--

OHMYGOD, I KNOW WHO YOU ARE!

AAGH! SHIT!

JUST KIDDING--

DAMN... DON'T DO THAT--

--I--

NO, SERIOUSLY, I KNOW WHO YOU ARE, YOU'RE DAN DREIBERG.

SHIT! NO! HOW? SHIT!

WE MET AT A PARTY A YEAR AGO... I WAS WITH THE OWNER OF A BIG MANUFACTURING COMPANY... YOU WERE BUYING PARTS FOR SOME SCIENTIFIC THING YOU WERE WORKING ON AND YOUR FACE STUCK IN MY HEAD--

CRAP-CRAP-CRAP--

IT'S OKAY... YOUR SECRET IS SAFE WITH ME. I GIVE YOU MY WORD, I'LL NEVER TELL ANYONE. EVER.

YOU GIVE ME YOUR WORD, HUH?

YES...AND ANYTHING ELSE YOU WANT.

THE NIGHT MY FATHER HAD THE HEART ATTACK THAT KILLED HIM, I COUNTED TO FIVE BEFORE I CALLED THE AMBULANCE.

WHAT I DID WAS WRONG.

YES, IT WAS.

YOU SHOULD'VE COUNTED TO *TEN*.

IT DOESN'T CHANGE THE FACT THAT YOU'RE A PROTECTOR. I COULD FEEL IT THE NIGHT WE MET, WHEN YOUR FRIEND CAME AFTER ME...IN YOUR VOICE WHEN YOU TALKED ABOUT FINDING THAT WOMAN.

YOU'RE A *GOOD MAN*, DANIEL... AND YOU'RE BEAUTIFUL...THE KIND OF BEAUTY THAT COMES FROM DEEP INSIDE. VERY, VERY BEAUTIFUL.

I... ...I SHOULD GO.

THERE'S THAT WORD AGAIN.

I'LL LET YOU KNOW WHAT I FIND ON THE PHONE NUMBERS AND--

LIZ.

WHAT?

LIZ. ELIZABETH LANE. IT'S MY NAME. SEEMS ONLY FAIR THAT YOU HAVE IT.

HI...GLAD TO MEET YOU.

AND I'M *VERY* GLAD TO MEET *YOU*...AND TO BE YOUR *FIRST*.

NO...I MEAN, WHAT'RE YOU TALKING ABOUT? I'VE HAD PLENTY OF--

A WOMAN *KNOWS* THESE THINGS, DAN.

DON'T FORGET YOUR CODPIECE.

OH JEEZ--

NOT THAT YOU NEED IT.

OH JEEZ--

"YOU LOOK EXHAUSTED, DAN."

YOU KNOW ME, HOLLIS, ALWAYS UP ALL NIGHT WORKING.

YOU ON A CASE?

YEAH. I MEAN, MAYBE. WE'LL SEE.

THREE ANSWERS TO ONE QUESTION. *IMPRESSIVE.*

I'M RUNNING DOWN SOME PHONE NUMBERS ON A...*POSSIBLE* CASE. MOST OF THEM HAVE TURNED INTO DEAD ENDS, BUT ONE OF THEM LED TO A PAY PHONE DOWNTOWN.

WHICH MEANS IT'S *ANOTHER* DEAD END--

"-- SINCE *ANYBODY* COULD'VE USED THAT PHONE. YOU NEED ROUND-THE-CLOCK SURVEILLANCE, WHICH WE DON'T HAVE. YOU'VE GOT NOTHING."

"NOT NECESSARILY."

I'VE FOUND A MOLECULAR POLYMER EXTRACT THAT MAY LET ME SEPARATE THE LAYERS OF OIL AND FINGERPRINTS THAT COVER THE RECEIVER.

THE POINT ISN'T TO SEE WHO USED THE PHONE, IT'S TO FIGURE OUT WHO'S USED IT A *LOT.* IF ONE PRINT APPEARS A LOT ON DIFFERENT LAYERS, THAT MAY BE MY TARGET.

I THOUGHT YOU SAID YOU WEREN'T GOING TO DRINK BEFORE NOON ANYMORE--

I'M NOT.

AH. OPTICAL ILLUSION, THEN...?

SOMETHING LIKE THAT.

I WAS THINKING ABOUT WHAT I SAID TO YOU THE OTHER DAY...ABOUT HOW IMPORTANT IT IS TO PROTECT THE NITE OWL NAME AND REPUTATION BY NOT DOING THE WRONG *THING*, OR BEING SEEN WITH THE WRONG *PEOPLE*, AND I REALIZED--

--I'M A HYPOCRITE.

HOLLIS, C'MON, YOU'RE NOT--

HEAR ME OUT.

THERE'S STUFF I'VE NEVER TOLD YOU, THAT I'VE NEVER TOLD *ANYONE*, THAT---MIGHT CHANGE THE WAY YOU AND EVERYBODY ELSE THINKS ABOUT ME. BUT I'VE BEEN THINKING, MAYBE IT'S TIME TO STOP BEING A HYPOCRITE AND TELL THE TRUTH.

THE THING ABOUT TRUTH, DAN, IS THAT THERE'S NOT JUST ONE KIND. THERE'S *FIVE*.

THERE'S THE TRUTH YOU TELL TO CASUAL ACQUAINTANCES. THE TRUTH YOU TELL YOUR FRIENDS AND FAMILY. THE TRUTH YOU TELL TO ONLY A FEW PEOPLE IN YOUR LIFE.

THE TRUTH YOU TELL *YOURSELF*, TO HELP YOU GET THROUGH YOUR DAYS AND NIGHTS. *ESPECIALLY* THE NIGHTS. AND THEN--

--AND THEN THERE'S TRUTH NUMBER FIVE, THE TRUTH YOU DON'T WANT TO ADMIT EVEN TO YOURSELF.

THAT'S WHAT *THIS* IS, DAN... TRUTH NUMBER FIVE. WROTE IT UP FOR YOU. WHAT YOU DO WITH IT IS UP TO YOU. YOU CAN TOSS IT OUT WITHOUT READING IT IF YOU DON'T WANT TO KNOW. BUT IF YOU *DO* READ IT--

I'LL LEAVE IT TO YOU TO DECIDE WHAT NEEDS TO BE DONE...ABOUT *IT* AND ABOUT *ME*...AND MAYBE THE PRICE I'LL NEED TO PAY FOR WHAT I'VE DONE.

I'LL SEE YOU ON THE OTHER SIDE OF THAT DECISION.

C'MON, IT CAN'T BE *THAT* BAD. NOTHING THAT COULD CHANGE THE WAY I LOOK AT YOU.

SO WHY ARE MY HANDS SHAKING?

CRAP!

OKAY, THIS IS RIDICULOUS. AND IT ISN'T ANY OF MY BUSINESS. JUST PUT THEM BACK IN THE ENVELOPE AND--

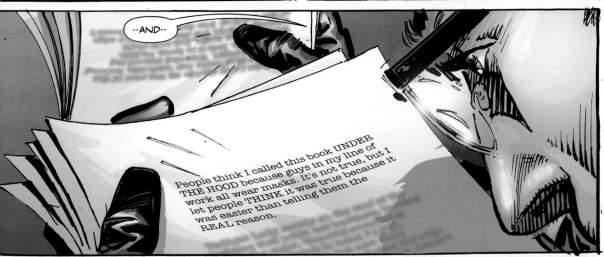

--AND--

People think I called this book UNDER THE HOOD because guys in my line of work all wear masks. It's not true, but I let people THINK it was true because it was easier than telling them the REAL reason.

Which is what I saw the night I finally looked under the mask of someone I considered my enemy...and glimpsed not just HIS face...but MY face... my TRUE face.

On that night, I realized that I'm not the man I thought I was. I'm not a hero. I'm not any KIND of a hero.

And maybe I need to be punished for what I've done. This is what happened.

...OH MY GOD....

...OH MY GOD...

...OH MY GOD....

"GOD'S SPIRIT IS STRONG IN THIS PLACE."

WE'RE VERY CLOSE TO LOCKING DOWN A TV CHANNEL OF OUR OWN, TO CARRY THE WORD TO MILLIONS OF VIEWERS AROUND THE COUNTRY. YOUR DOLLARS COULD MAKE THAT HAPPEN.

WELL, WE'RE CERTAINLY IMPRESSED. IF WE CAN JUST HAVE A WORD--

OF COURSE.

I'LL GET OUT OF YOUR WAY, I WAS JUST LEAVING--

THANK YOU. OH, AND IF YOU COULD DO ONE THING FOR ME ON YOUR WAY OUT--

--THERE'RE SOME BOXES IN THE SUBBASEMENT I NEED MOVED UP TO MY OFFICE. THEY'RE CLEARLY MARKED. IF YOU COULD BRING THEM UP--

I THOUGHT YOU NEVER LET ANYBODY DOWN THERE.

YES, BUT YOU'RE NOT JUST ANYBODY. YOU'RE MY GOOD AND FAITHFUL SERVANT.

NOW, IF THE REST OF YOU COULD JUST COME THIS WAY, I HAVE SOME PAMPHLETS YOU SHOULD READ.

...HELP ME...
PLEASE...

...PLEASE....

NITE OWL

"LET IT BURN..."

WHEN I FIRST REALIZED **WHO** YOU WERE, AND **WHAT** YOU WERE, I THOUGHT YOU WERE SENT BY THE DEVIL TO INTERFERE WITH GOD'S PLANS.

THEN I UNDERSTOOD THAT YOU WERE INDEED SENT BY GOD TO **AID** HIS PLANS, TO **FINISH** THE WORK WE HAD BEGUN.

TO SEND THE WORLD A **MESSAGE** IN A PILLAR OF **FLESH** AND **CORRUPTION.**

A PILLAR OF **FIRE** AND **SMOKE.**

A BONFIRE OF **SIN** INCARNATE.

SO WHAT DID YOU FIND?

⌐ROM ONE NITE OWL TO ANOTHER

MICHAEL STRACZYNSKI—WRITER • **ANDY KUBERT**—PENCILS
BILL SIENKIEWICZ—INKS • **BRAD ANDERSON**—COLORS • **NICK NAPOLITANO**—LETTERS
CAMILLA ZHANG — ASST. EDITOR • **MARK DOYLE** — ASSOC. EDITOR • **WILL DENNIS** — EDITOR
ANDY KUBERT, BILL SIENKIEWICZ & BRAD ANDERSON—COVER • **ETHAN VAN SCIVER & HI-FI** VARIANT COVER

ONE SET OF FINGERPRINTS SHOWED UP SEVERAL TIMES ON THE PHONE BOOTH VINCENT CALLED TO SELL OFF HIS GIRLS ONCE HE DECIDED THEY WERE USED UP.

I CHECKED THEM AGAINST THE POLICE AND EMPLOYMENT DATABASES AND TURNED UP A GUY NAMED "TAYLOR DEAN."

AS IN *REVEREND* TAYLOR DEAN?

YEAH. PROBLEM IS, HIS CHURCH WORKS THE STREETS IN THAT AREA, SO IT MAY BE COMPLETELY INNOCENT--

NO ONE IS "COMPLETELY INNOCENT."

"I KNOW...

"...BELIEVE ME, I KNOW."

THAT'S WHY WE'RE GOING TO PAY HIM A VISIT ANYWAY, JUST TO BE SAFE--

"--ASSUMING HE'S NOT ASLEEP IN BED BY NOW."

I WANT YOU TO KNOW THE **TRUTH**, WALTER, SO YOU WILL **UNDERSTAND** THAT YOU ARE DYING IN A WORTHY CAUSE. THE IDEA CAME UNEXPECTEDLY, AS ALL SUCH IDEAS DO...FROM A HIGHER POWER.

"SHE COST TWO HUNDRED DOLLARS. FULL SERVICE. NOT TOO MUCH, NOT TOO CHEAP. ECONOMICAL. AT LEAST THAT'S WHAT I **THOUGHT**.

--AND I WAS WATCHING THE NEWS LAST NIGHT--

--ROBERT--

--AND I SAW A **STORY** ABOUT HOW THIS GUY NAMED **REVEREND DEAN** WAS PROTESTING OUTSIDE A **PORN** SHOP. INTERVIEWED HIM AND EVERYTHING.

I... LOOK, I SHOULD GO, I'M LATE FOR--

AND I THOUGHT, WHY, THAT'S MY BOUNCEBUDDY **ROBERT**...AND **THEN** I THOUGHT--

--I WONDER WHAT THEY'D **THINK** IF THEY **KNEW** WHAT YOU AND I WERE **DOING** UP HERE TWICE A WEEK.

I IMAGINE ALL THOSE **RICH** FOLKS GIVING YOU ALL THAT **MONEY** FOR THAT **CHURCH** DOWNTOWN WOULD BE VERY **DISAPPOINTED**--

YOU CAN'T DO THIS TO ME--

OH, YES I CAN, SWEETIE. YOU'RE GOING TO PAY ME ONE **THOUSAND** DOLLARS A WEEK UNTIL I SAY OTHERWISE OR--

NO! I WON'T LET YOU DESTROY EVERYTHING I'VE BUILT! HARLOT! I WON'T LET YOU! I WON'T LET YOU!

UCCHHHHH--

I-- --I-- OH GOD...OGOD, WHAT HAVE I DONE?

"WHAT I'D **DONE** WAS JUST THE **BEGINNING**."

"I SET THE APARTMENT ON FIRE TO DESTROY ANY **EVIDENCE** AND MAKE IT HARDER TO PROVE THAT SHE'D BEEN **MURDERED**.

"STILL, I GOT READY TO LEAVE TOWN, FIGURING THAT THIS WOULD ONLY **DELAY** THE INEVITABLE. BUT I WAS WRONG.

"ONCE THE NEIGHBORS LEARNED JUST WHAT SORT OF WOMAN HAD BEEN RENTING AN APARTMENT IN THEIR BUILDING, THEY WERE **SCANDALIZED**.

WATCH

"THEY EVICTED A COUPLE OF OTHERS NEXT DOOR, SET UP A NEIGHBORHOOD WATCH PROGRAM--

"--CLEANED THE WHOLE PLACE RIGHT UP."

THE BIBLE SAYS "THE *WAGES OF SIN ARE DEATH.*" THAT'S A WARNING, WALTER. YOU WANT TO KEEP SIN FAR AWAY, BECAUSE IF YOU SIN, YOU DIE. FOREVER.

IN FIRE.

IF THE BODY OF **ONE** SINNER BURNED IN HELL'S FIRE COULD DO SO MUCH GOOD, HOW MUCH **MORE** COULD BE DONE BY A WHOLE **PILE** OF THEM? THINK OF THE **MESSAGE** THAT WOULD SEND.

A PILE OF **CORRUPTION** GONE TO FLAME IN THE BASEMENT OF GOD'S HOUSE...THE CONTRAST BETWEEN THE PURE AND THE PROFANE...WHAT AN IMAGE.

SO I WENT TO WORK.

YOUNG HARLOTS. OLDER ONES. YOUNG MEN. DIDN'T MATTER, THEY WERE ALL **USEFUL**, ALL **FUEL** FOR THE **FLAMES**.

AFTER I WAS **DONE** WITH THEM, OF COURSE.

THE MORE I DID, IT THE MORE I **ENJOYED** DOING IT. I WAS **GOOD** AT IT. I **LIKED** IT.

FOR A WHILE I EVEN ENJOYED THE RISK OF BRINGING THE BODIES *BACK* HERE, BUT I KNEW GOD WOULDN'T LET ME BE CAUGHT. I WAS DOING GOD'S WORK.

BUT I STILL HAD TO LEAVE MY *LAST* TASK EARLY, WHEN I FEARED SOMEONE MIGHT HAVE HEARD HER *SCREAMS* AND CALLED THE POLICE.

SLOPPY. UNFORTUNATE. STILL, HER HANDCUFFS PROVIDED A NICE WAY OF HANDLING *YOU,* WALTER.

I KNEW GOD WOULD SEND SOMEONE TO TAKE THE *BLAME* FOR WHAT I'D DONE, SOMEONE AS CORRUPT AS THE BODIES HE WOULD BE *FOUND* WITH...THE BODIES HE WOULD BE HELD *RESPONSIBLE* FOR.

BECAUSE ACCIDENTS HAPPEN TO PEOPLE LIKE YOU, WALTER.

YOUR ABUSE OF THIS SACRED TEMPLE WILL BE MY CLARION CALL. ON THE ASHES OF YOU AND YOUR FELLOW SINNERS WE WILL BUILD A NEW CHURCH, A *BIGGER* CHURCH.

MEANWHILE I'LL FIND SOMEWHERE *ELSE* TO STORE THE BODIES I NEED FOR THE *NEXT* MESSAGE.

BECAUSE AS FOUR GOSPELS AND SIXTY-TWO *OTHER* BOOKS IN THE BIBLE CONFIRM, THERE'S *ALWAYS* ANOTHER MESSAGE IN NEED OF SENDING.

SHOULD BE ALMOST IN VIEW BY NOW.

YOU KNOW, SOMEDAY THEY'LL HAVE SATELLITE TRACKERS THAT WILL SHOW YOUR POSITION TO WITHIN A FEW FEET OF--

THERE.

WHERE?

FOLLOW THE SMOKE.

SEX-SHOP HANDCUFFS... CHEAP METAL... NOT REGULATION STEEL.

LET IT BURN.

ARRGHHHH!

WE NEED TO SPLIT UP, LOOK FOR ANYONE TRAPPED INSIDE. YOU GO UP, I'LL GO DOWN.

TURNS OUT THAT *IS* YOUR SPECIALTY--

OHJEEZ--

I *SO* LOVE DOING THAT TO HIM.

HELLO? ANYONE HERE? HELLO?

COME ON... COME ON... COME--

--ON

IS ANYONE THERE?

OWL... THAT YOU?

RORSCHACH? WHAT'RE YOU--

DISCUSS LATER...OPEN THE GODDAMN DOOR!

OKAY, STAND BACK!

FIRE IN THE HOLE!

YOU ALL RIGHT?

YES. NO. DOESN'T MATTER.

SO YOU TRACKED DEAN HERE TOO, THEN?

SOMETHING LIKE THAT.

BUT WHAT'S INSIDE THE--

OHMYGOD...

WHAT HAPPENED? WHAT WAS HE--

RORSCHACH?

RORSCHACH?

TAKE A LETTER, MARIA...WON'T BE COMING HOME--

YOU SEEM AWFULLY CALM FOR SOMEONE WHOSE CHURCH IS BURNING DOWN.

THE
END
IS
NIGH

ONCE YOU REALIZE THAT EVERYTHING IS PART OF GOD'S PLAN, VERY LITTLE WORRIES YOU ANYMORE.

IS THAT WHAT YOU TOLD THE WOMEN YOU KILLED?

DON'T KNOW WHAT YOU'RE TALKING ABOUT, MA'AM. OR IS IT MISS? OR MIZZ?

IT'S CERTAINLY NOT LADY...NOT DRESSED LIKE THAT.

SLUT? ALMOST CERTAINLY.

HOLY BIBLE
PSALMS

BLAM BLAM BLAM

WHERE--

RIGHT HERE!

UNNH!

THINK YOU'RE SO SMART...THINK YOU'RE GOOD ENOUGH TO FIGHT A MAN--

WHEN I SEE ONE...I'LL LET YOU KNOW.

SHOW YOU WHAT A REAL MAN DOES TO A WOMAN--

NO--

LET HIM SEE HOW A REAL MAN BEHAVES--

NO--

THAT'S ENOUGH--

--THAT'S GODDAMNED WELL ENOUGH!

GONNA SHOW YOU WHAT HAPPENS TO A **WHORE,** WHAT--

--WHAT ARE **YOU** SMILING ABOUT?

I CAN **SEE**--

SEE WHAT? SEE GOD? SEE THE END OF YOUR LIFE? WHAT DO YOU **SEE,** SLUT?

BEHIND YOU.

NO--

THE END IS NIGH

RORSCHACH, **NO!**

EEEAAAGH!

THAT--

--THAT'S WHAT HAPPENS TO A WHORE.

THE END IS NIGH

THE END IS NIGH

THE END IS NIGH

WHAT DID YOU DO? *WHAT DID* YOU DO?

WHAT YOU WOULDN'T.

WHAT YOU *COULDN'T.*

HOWEVER MUCH YOU WANTED TO.

YOU CAN'T DO THIS...WE *TALKED* ABOUT THIS--

YES. TALK. IT'S WHAT YOU'RE GOOD AT. YOU TALK. I'LL DO. GOOD PARTNERSHIP.

NO, I--

GENTLEMEN--

--ONE, THE JOINT IS STILL ON FIRE. TWO, I HEAR POLICE SIRENS. THREE--

--NO, ACTUALLY, I DON'T *NEED* A "THREE" AFTER *FIRE* AND *POLICE.*

OKAY, FINE, I--

RORSCHACH? RORSCHACH?

WE HAVE TO GO... NOW!

THE END IS NIGH

"-- WHERE THE BODY OF REVEREND TAYLOR STONE WAS FOUND WITH TWENTY-SEVEN MURDER VICTIMS AMID THE CHARRED REMAINS OF HIS CHURCH."

AS YOU CAN SEE, I MADE MY DECISION.

SO YOU READ IT?

YES, AND I DON'T *CARE* WHAT HAPPENED IN THE PAST, I KNOW THE PERSON YOU *ARE*.

THE PERSON I NEEDED YOU TO *BE*.

THE WAY THE WHOLE *COUNTRY* STILL NEEDS YOU TO BE...A HERO.

I'M NOT--

JUST *LISTEN* TO ME.

YOU'RE THE CLOSEST THING I'VE EVER HAD TO A FATHER, A *REAL* FATHER. WHEN I USED TO GET THE CRAP KICKED OUT OF ME AS A KID, THE ONLY THING THAT KEPT ME GOING WAS KNOWING THAT THERE WERE GUYS LIKE YOU IN THE WORLD, WHO NEVER *EVER* GAVE UP.

AND I DOUBT I'M THE *ONLY* ONE.

DON'T DO THIS. PLEASE.

I'LL MAKE A DEAL WITH YOU.

I HAVE A COPY OF THIS IN MY SAFETY DEPOSIT BOX. I'LL LEAVE IT THERE. WHEN I'M DEAD, WHEN I DON'T HAVE TO BE THE GUY YOU AND EVERYBODY ELSE THINKS I NEED TO BE, YOU CAN REVISIT YOUR DECISION.

THEN I WON'T HAVE TO WORRY ABOUT IT FOR A LONG TIME, BECAUSE YOU'RE NOT GOING ANYWHERE.

MAYBE...MAYBE NOT. BUT YOU'RE RIGHT. DOESN'T MATTER WHETHER YOU WIN OR LOSE. ALL THAT MATTERS, WHEN THE TIME COMES--

--IS THAT YOU GO DOWN SWINGING.

I SHOULD TURN YOU IN TO THE POLICE, YOU *KNOW* THAT, RIGHT?

IF WE'D LET HIM *GO* HE WOULD'VE WALKED. MONEY. POWER. EXPENSIVE ATTORNEYS. WOULDN'T EVEN HAVE BEEN *CLOSE*.

YOU CAN'T JUST KILL PEOPLE--

YOU *SAW* WHAT HE DID--

I WOULD'VE--

YOU WOULD'VE *NOTHING*.

IF YOU WERE GOING TO *DO* SOMETHING YOU WOULD'VE DONE IT WHEN YOUR *DAD* WAS BEATING YOUR *MOTHER*--

STOP IT--

--BUT YOU WERE SOFT, LIKE YOU'RE SOFT NOW, BECAUSE WOMEN MAKE YOU SOFT, MAKE YOU *HESITATE*--

YEAH, YOU AND ME, WE'RE GONNA START ALL *OVER*...JUST GOTTA DEAL WITH THE *BRAT* IS ALL.

LITTLE ACCIDENT...KIDS HAVE 'EM ALL THE TIME. YEAH...GONNA HAVE A LATE TERM-- *REALLY* LATE TERM-- ABORTION.

WHAT THE--

AAAAAIIIII!

"SOMETIMES TO MAKE THINGS RIGHT YOU HAVE TO DO THINGS *WRONG.* I'M WILLING TO *DO* THOSE THINGS. I'VE *ALWAYS* BEEN WILLING TO DO THEM--"

--AND YOU'RE **NOT**.

I THINK WE NEED TO TAKE A BREAK FROM EACH OTHER FOR A WHILE, RORSCHACH. A COUPLE OF WEEKS...WE'LL SEE.

SO YOU'RE NOT CALLING THE POLICE?

"NO...AT LEAST, NOT **THIS** TIME. BECAUSE WE'RE ALL ENTITLED TO ONE REALLY BIG MISTAKE."

AUTO REPAIRS

CLOSED

WE FIX 'EM!

OBSOLETE MODELS A SPECIALTY.

ONE MISTAKE. RIGHT.

BUT IS IT YOURS OR MINE?

ELIZABETH...? LIZ?

I THOUGHT WE MIGHT GO OUT, GET SOME--

--DINNER...?

"HMMM. WHAT'S THIS?"

From one 'Night Bird' to Another. Love from The Twilight Lady

THAT? OH, THAT ISN'T ANYBODY. IT'S JUST THIS *VICE QUEEN* I PUT AWAY BACK IN '68. CALLED HERSELF *DUSK WOMAN* OR SOMETHING.

"THE TWILIGHT LADY. SHE SENT YOU HER *PICTURE?*"

"YEAH, WELL, I GUESS SHE HAD SORT OF A--

"-- FIXATION."

HA-HA-! I CAN'T BELIEVE YOU WANTED TO WEAR YOUR MASK--

STOP--

YOU LOOKED SO SILLY..."*I AM THE NITE OWL, FEAR ME, BABY! MOUNT ME!*"

YOU'RE A VERY SICK WOMAN--

"SHE WAS A VERY SICK WOMAN."

I KEPT MEANING TO THROW THAT PICTURE AWAY, BUT YOU KNOW HOW IT IS...

"HELLO? IS SOMEONE THERE?"

ARE YOU--

--YOU'RE THERE, AREN'T YOU? WHY WON'T YOU TALK TO ME? WHY WON'T YOU SAY SOMETHING? WHY WON'T YOU--

--WHY WON'T YOU SEE ME?

BECAUSE--

--BECAUSE I CAN AFFORD ANYTHING, DAN.

I CAN AFFORD CARS, AND JEWELS, AND SEX TOYS, AND EVERYTHING A WOMAN--

--A WOMAN IN MY PROFESSION--

--COULD EVER WANT.

THERE'S ONLY ONE THING IN THE WHOLE WORLD THAT I CAN'T AFFORD, DAN.

END

DR. MANHATTAN

"I WATCH AS A BOX CONTAINING A MYSTERY IS LOWERED INTO THE SOIL."

THOU KNOWEST, LORD, THE SECRETS OF OUR HEARTS;

SHUT NOT THY MERCIFUL EARS TO OUR PRAYERS, BUT SPARE US, LORD MOST HOLY, O GOD MOST MIGHTY, O HOLY AND MERCIFUL SAVIOR--

--THOU MOST WORTHY JUDGE ETERNAL, SUFFER US NOT, AT OUR LAST HOUR--

--FOR ANY PAINS OF DEATH, TO FALL FROM THEE.

AMEN.

I WATCH AS A BOX CONTAINING A MYSTERY IS LOWERED INTO THE SOIL. OF THOSE ATTENDING, I AM THE ONLY ONE WHO UNDERSTANDS THAT ALL BOXES ARE MYSTERIES, CONTAINING UNIVERSES.

GERMANY, AUGUST 14TH, 1938. I AM NINE YEARS OLD. I AM UNWRAPPING A BIRTHDAY PRESENT FROM MY FATHER.

QUANTUM PHYSICS SAYS THAT AS LONG AS THE BOX IS CLOSED, IT COULD CONTAIN ANYTHING, IN ANY STATE OF EXISTENCE.

WOW!

WOW!

WOW!

WOW!

THE OBSERVER AFFECTS THE OBSERVED, AT EACH STEP CREATING NEW UNIVERSES, NEW POSSIBILITIES.

IN OTHER QUANTUM PROBABILITIES, MY FATHER GAVE ME WOODEN SOLDIERS, A TOY CASTLE, CONSTRUCTION BLOCKS--

--BUT IN THIS QUANTUM UNIVERSE, *THIS* WAS INSIDE THE BOX.

A CLOCK...IT'S BEAUTIFUL!

YOUR MOTHER THINKS IT'S A BIT MUCH FOR A NINE-YEAR-OLD...

...BUT I THINK IT WILL HELP YOU UNDERSTAND THAT TIME HAS WEIGHT AND POWER--

"--THE POWER TO CHANGE LIVES. EVEN A SECOND CAN MAKE THE DIFFERENCE BETWEEN LIFE AND DEATH."

IT'S AUGUST 20TH, 1959. I'M ENTERING THE TEST CHAMBER IN THE INTRINSIC FIELD CENTER. I ASSUME I HAVE TIME TO GET MY COAT.

I'M WRONG.

ONE SECOND BECOMES ZERO.

00:04

OPERATING

THE PRESENT IS WRAPPED.

WHAT'S INSIDE THE BOX?

JUST A LITTLE MORE--

OW!

WHAT THE--

ACCIDENTS HAPPEN. THAT'S WHAT EVERYONE SAYS.

BUT IN A QUANTUM UNIVERSE THERE ARE NO SUCH THINGS AS ACCIDENTS, ONLY POSSIBILITIES AND PROBABILITIES FOLDED INTO EXISTENCE BY PERCEPTION.

IT'S OCTOBER, 1985. THE PHOTOGRAPH IS IN MY HAND. TWELVE SECONDS FROM NOW, IT FALLS AND FLUTTERS TO THE DRY MARTIAN GROUND. I'M LOOKING AT ME LOOKING AT ME--

--THROUGH THE CAMERA LENS WHERE IT'S JULY, 1959, RIGHT NOW.

ME LOOKING AT ME LOOKING AT ME, ALL HAPPENING AT THE SAME TIME. PROOF, I SUPPOSE, THAT I AM.

BUT THE QUESTION IS: WHY AM I?

ACCIDENTS HAPPEN.

EXCEPT THEY DON'T.

SO WHY AM I WHAT I AM?

WHAT'S IN THE BOX?

J. MICHAEL STRACZYNSKI script   ADAM HUGHES art
LAURA MARTIN colors   STEVE WANDS letters   ADAM HUGHES cover
PAUL POPE with LOVERN KINDZIERSKI and JIM LEE with SCOTT WILLIAMS & ALEX SINCLAIR variant covers
CAMILLA ZHANG asst. editor   CHRIS CONROY assoc. editor   MARK CHIARELLO editor
WATCHMEN created by ALAN MOORE and DAVE GIBBONS

JUNE, 1960. THE GROUP OF HEROES KNOWN AS THE MINUTEMEN ARE HOLDING A FUNDRAISER TO COMBAT FAMINE IN INDIA.

I'D TOLD PRESIDENT RAJENDRA PRASAD THAT I COULD SIMPLY CHANGE THE NITROGEN CONTENT IN THE TOPSOIL TO MAKE THE LAND FERTILE, SO THEY COULD GROW ANYTHING THEY WANTED.

HELP FEED THE HUNGRY IN INDIA

HE COULDN'T UNDERSTAND THE CONCEPT. THE SCALE WAS TOO BIG. IT DIDN'T FIT IN HIS BOX.

YOU DON'T AGE, DO YOU?

THIS IS MY PERCEPTION OF MYSELF. MY PERCEPTION DOES NOT CHANGE, HENCE MY APPEARANCE DOES NOT CHANGE OR AGE.

WELL, *THAT* MUST BE HANDY.

WISH I COULD DO THAT. I'M TEN YEARS OLDER AND TWENTY POUNDS FATTER THAN I IMAGINE MYSELF. EVERY MORNING I LOOK IN THE MIRROR AND THINK *HOW THE HELL DID THAT FAT OLD GUY GET IN HERE?* THEN I REALIZE IT'S ME.

SOMETIMES...WELL, TONIGHT...I THINK, MAYBE I SHOULD JUST WALK AWAY.

WHAT WOULD YOU DO INSTEAD?

FIX CARS. CAN YOU IMAGINE THAT?

THERE'S SOMETHING ABOUT *FIXING* THINGS THAT...I DON'T KNOW, MAKES ME FEEL GOOD. MAYBE THAT'S WHY WE GOT INTO ALL THIS...*STUFF*...IN THE FIRST PLACE. TO FIX THINGS. TO FIX THE *WORLD.*

BUT I CAN'T.

I WANT TO FORCE CARS TO WORK BECAUSE I CAN'T FORCE THE UNIVERSE TO MAKE SENSE--

"--CAN'T CONTROL EVERYTHING."

ARE YOU *EVER* GOING TO STOP FIXING THOSE THINGS?

MARCH 3RD, 1949.

IT'S A *BEAUTIFUL* DAY OUTSIDE. SOME OF THE OTHERS WANT TO HIKE DOWN TO THE LAKE. THEY INVITED ME AND THEY *EVEN* INVITED *YOU.*

THEY *SAID* YOU WOULDN'T COME BUT I SAID YOU *WOULD* IF SOMEONE JUST *ASKED* YOU.

THEY THINK YOU'RE *STUFFY,* THAT YOU'RE TOO *ORGANIZED,* TOO *NARROW,* THAT YOU DON'T KNOW HOW TO HAVE *FUN,* OR BE *SPONTANEOUS.*

WELL, I SAY THEY'RE *WRONG.* YOU JUST NEED TO BE GIVEN A *CHANCE,* A *REASON,* AN *OPENING* SO YOU CAN BE *SURPRISED* BY *LIFE* ONCE IN A WHILE.

SO? ARE YOU COMING *WITH US* OR *NOT?*

I CAN'T. I HAVE TO FINISH THIS.

FINE. SUIT YOURSELF. I HOPE YOU AND YOUR GEARS WILL BE VERY HAPPY TOGETHER.

SYMMETRY.

ORDER.

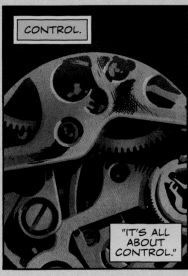

CONTROL.

"IT'S ALL ABOUT CONTROL."

MAY 12th, 1959. GILA FLATS. PROFESSOR GLASS IS WELCOMING ME TO GILA FLATS.

OPPENHEIMER AND THOSE GUYS AT THE MANHATTAN PROJECT SHOWED US ATOMIC POWER CAN DESTROY THE WORLD.

OUR JOB IS TO FIGURE OUT HOW TO *CONTROL* ATOMIC POWER SO IT CAN *CHANGE* THE WORLD. GLAD TO HAVE YOU WITH US, JON.

SHOW HIM AROUND, WALLY.

YES, SIR.

THIS IS WHERE THEY'RE DOING *INTRINSIC FIELD EXPERIMENTS.* IT'S LIKE, WHAT IF THERE'S SOME *FIELD* HOLDING STUFF *TOGETHER* APART FROM *GRAVITY?*

THIS IS OUR TIME-LOCK *TEST VAULT,* SO THAT WHEN THEY'RE TRYIN' TO SEPARATE *OBJECTS* FROM THEIR *INTRINSIC FIELDS* NO RADIATION GETS OUT.

WE GOTTA *LOT* OF NEW SAFETY FEATURES LIKE THAT HERE.

I'LL SHOW YOU WHERE THE *REAL* HEAVY DUTY THINKIN' GETS DONE AROUND HERE. WE CALL IT THE *BESTIARY,* IT'S OVER IN BUILDING SIX.

AS WALLY STEERS ME INTO THE ROOM, I FEEL A SUDDEN SENSATION OF *DÉJÀ VU.* I'VE SEEN THIS PLACE BEFORE--

--EXCEPT THAT IT WAS *DESERTED* THEN, DERELICT, WITH STARLIGHT SHINING DOWN UPON ITS ROTTED FLOORBOARDS, THROUGH THE COLLAPSED CEILING.

AND IN THAT MOMENT--

AND IN THAT MOMENT--

AND IN THIS AND EVERY MOMENT IN BETWEEN, I WONDER...HOW IS THAT POSSIBLE?

I HAD NOT YET CHANGED INTO WHAT I AM NOW. BUT I COULD STILL **SENSE** MYSELF IN THE FUTURE.

BECAUSE IT WAS STILL **ME**, STILL MY CONSCIOUSNESS, SLIDING UP AND DOWN THE TIMESTREAM.

STILL THE SAME QUANTUM OBSERVER.

EVEN AS I THINK THESE WORDS FOR THE FIRST TIME, THE **ME** WHO IS MY FUTURE SELF IS **REMEMBERING** ME THINKING THESE WORDS FOR THE FIRST TIME.

THERE IS A LINE THAT CONNECTS US. BUT HOW FAR BACK DOES THAT LINE GO?

AND IS THAT FUTURE ME THE **SAME** FUTURE ME THAT WOULD HAVE EXISTED HAD I NOT MADE CERTAIN DECISIONS, CERTAIN--

--CHANGES?

"I GUESS I SHOULD **WELCOME** EVERYBODY TO THE FIRST EVER MEETING OF THE **CRIMEBUSTERS.**"

1966.

IF CRIMEBUSTERS IS TO BECOME AN EFFICIENT CRIME-FIGHTING ORGANIZATION, IT'S IMPORTANT THAT WE LEARN TO WORK TOGETHER.

BURRUP.

WHAT'S THE MATTER?

YOU WERE STARING AT THAT *GIRL* IS THE MATTER! NOW PAY *ATTENTION.*

I'D LIKE TO START BY PAIRING PEOPLE UP INTO GROUPS OF TWO, SO WE CAN LEARN ABOUT EACH OTHER'S IDEAS, GOALS, AND WHAT WE HOPE TO ACHIEVE WITH CRIMEBUSTERS. THAT'S WHY I HAD EACH OF YOU PUT YOUR I.D. ON A SLIP OF PAPER.

WHAT'S IN THE BOX?

OUR FIRST IS DR. MANHATTAN, WHOSE PRESENCE HERE TONIGHT HONORS ALL OF US--

IT'S ALL A MATTER OF PERSPECTIVE.

--AND THE ONE HE'S PARTNERED WITH TONIGHT IS--

AND PERSPECTIVES CAN BE CHANGED...WITH THE SLIGHTEST NUDGE.

--IS--

--THE SILK SPECTRE.

AND A NEW QUANTUM UNIVERSE OF EVENTS AND POTENTIALITIES IS CREATED IN AN INSTANT...

Silk Spect

...BORN IN THE SPLIT BETWEEN WHAT *MIGHT* HAVE BEEN AND WHAT NOW *IS*.

IN THAT INSTANT, THE FUTURE ME THAT WOULD HAVE WORKED WITH RORSCHACH CEASED TO EXIST AND BECAME THE ME THAT WORKED WITH LAURIE...THAT *LOVED* LAURIE....

"JON, I THINK I'D LIKE TO *GO HOME* NOW, PLEASE."

WHAT?

I SAID I WANT TO GO HOME NOW.

PLEASE! DON'T ALL LEAVE--

JANEY--

I SAW THE WAY YOU WERE LOOKING AT HER. CHEAP, TRASHY JAILBAIT!

YOU DID SOMETHING, SO YOU'D BE ASSIGNED TO HER, DIDN'T YOU?

NO. IN THIS QUANTUM REALITY, I WAS ALWAYS PAIRED UP WITH HER TONIGHT.

THE STATEMENT WAS TRUE. IT WAS ALSO UTTERLY BESIDE THE POINT.

IT'S BECAUSE I'M GETTING OLDER, ISN'T IT? YOU WANT SOMEONE YOUNGER, DON'T YOU?

I LOVE YOU, JANEY.

THE STATEMENT WAS TRUE. IT, TOO, WAS UTTERLY BESIDE THE POINT.

TAKE ME HOME... JUST...TAKE ME HOME.

BEING HOME WOULD HELP, AT LEAST FOR A WHILE.

A CHANGE IN PERSPECTIVE.

A CHANGE IN PERSPECTIVE...

I JUST CAN'T DO THIS ANYMORE, DOC; I'M QUITTING. I NEED TO GET MY LIFE IN ORDER, FIGURE OUT WHO I AM BENEATH THE MASK.

--AND THE ARRIVAL OF YOUR POWER ON THE WORLD SCENE ASSURES AMERICA THAT OUR SOLDIERS NEED NOT GET INVOLVED IN SITUATIONS LIKE THAT IN VIETNAM--

I'M LEAVING YOU...

I LOVE YOU...

--SHAME ABOUT WHAT HAPPENED TO JACK, BUT AMERICA'S GOT ENEMIES WHO WON'T BE SPOOKED INTO SUBMISSION, THAT'S GONNA REQUIRE SOLDIERS AND TANKS AND GUNS AND, WELL, YOU, SON--

--AND I THINK WE'RE OFF TO A GOOD START, BUT WE CAN DO BETTER, COME UP WITH SOME NEW IDEAS--

HE DOESN'T HAVE WHAT IT TAKES... BETTER OFF BY MYSELF... SHOULD NEVER HAVE WORKED WITH ME IN THE FIRST PLACE, ALWAYS THOUGHT HE BELONGED WITH SILK SPECTRE--

ONE GEAR TURNS... IT TURNS ANOTHER, WHICH TURNS ANOTHER...BUT IT ALL STARTS WITH ONE TICK OF THE CLOCK, THE UNCOILING OF THE SPRING--

--THE FIRST GEAR WHOSE TURNING SET EVERYTHING ELSE IN MOTION.

WHY DID THE DOOR TO THE REACTION CHAMBER CLOSE WHEN I WAS *SURE* I HAD TIME?

WITH MY BODY BROKEN DOWN INTO AN INFINITY OF QUANTUM POSSIBILITIES, WITH EACH SUBSEQUENT CHOICE CREATING YET ANOTHER POSSIBILITY, ANOTHER *ME*, IN THE FINAL ANALYSIS, WHO *AM I?*

WHY AM I?

"I'M SORRY TO BRING YOU SUCH UNFORTUNATE NEWS, MR. OSTERMAN--

AUGUST, 1959.

--BUT THERE'S NOTHING WE CAN DO.

WE CAN HANDLE ALL THE ARRANGEMENTS FOR THE FUNERAL, EVEN THOUGH THERE'S NOTHING TECHNICALLY LEFT TO BURY--

MY SON...IS NOT DEAD.

MR. OSTERMAN--

MY SON IS NOT DEAD! IF YOU DID THIS TO HIM THEN YOU CAN FIX IT!

WE TRIED TO REVERSE THE INTRINSIC FIELD GENERATORS IN THE HOPE THAT IT MIGHT SOMEHOW RECREATE HIM, BUT--

NO!

YOU JUST NEED...TO FIND THE PIECES... AND PUT THEM TOGETHER...TO FIX HIM...

NOVEMBER 10TH, 1959.

"...ONE GEAR...THAT CONNECTS TO ANOTHER..."

NOVEMBER 14TH, 1959.

"...TO ANOTHER... AND THEN YOU TURN THE WATCH, AND..."

HE'S NOT DEAD...JUST HAVE TO FIX HIM--

FATHER...IT'S ME...I'M RIGHT HERE.

IT'S ME...IT'S JON.

DAD...? WHAT'S WRONG? WHAT'S--

GOD HELP ME...GOD IN HEAVEN...MY SON IS DEAD...MY SON IS GONE...

...THEY'VE TAKEN HIM FROM ME.

HE WAS RIGHT. IT TOOK ME YEARS TO SEE THAT, BUT IN THE END, HE WAS RIGHT.

I AM NOT JON, BUT JON *BECAME* ME. HIS PERSPECTIVE *INFORMED* ME, HIS PERSPECTIVE--

--CREATED ME? IS THAT POSSIBLE? WHAT HAPPENED IN THAT MOMENT, THAT SURGE OF ENERGY THAT RESULTED IN MY BIRTH? IF I AM A QUANTUM *EFFECT*, WHAT WAS THE QUANTUM *CAUSE*?

WHATEVER IT WAS, DID IT HAPPEN *BEFORE* THE INCIDENT, OR *DURING* THE INCIDENT?

WHAT'S IN THE BOX?

I KNOW THAT I CAN RIDE THE TIMELINE BACK AND FORTH BETWEEN THE FUTURE AND THE MOMENT OF MY CREATION...

...AND THE MOMENT OF DÉJÀ VU IN GILA FLATS SHOWS THAT EVEN BEFORE THE INCIDENT MY CONSCIOUSNESS WAS ABLE TO RIDE THE TIMELINE FORWARD PAST THE POINT OF MY BODY'S DESTRUCTION.

I'VE NEVER TRIED THE REVERSE...TO EXTEND MY CONSCIOUSNESS TO A POINT *BEFORE* MY CREATION, TO SEE IF I COULD EXPERIENCE THOSE MOMENTS NOT AS DEAD MEMORIES, BUT AS ALIVE AS THIS MOMENT. I ALWAYS THOUGHT IT WOULD BE LIKE THE UNIVERSE TRYING TO REMEMBER ITSELF BEFORE THE BIG BANG.

AND PERHAPS...IT IS TIME TO TRY.

GILA FLATS.

BACK FROM LUNCH EARLY, DR. OSTERMAN?

YEAH...LEFT JANEY'S WATCH IN MY COAT POCKET. JUST FIXED IT.

GOTTA GIVE IT TO YOU, DOC. SEEMS LIKE THERE'S NOTHING BROKEN SO BAD THAT YOU CAN'T PUT IT BACK TOGETHER AGAIN.

BUT...
IT'S NOT
POSSIBLE--

♪

IT'S ONE-FIFTEEN P.M.,
AUGUST 20TH, 1959.
THE MOMENT I WAS
BORN. THE MOMENT
OF THE ACCIDENT.

BECAUSE
ACCIDENTS HAPPEN.

EXCEPT THIS
ONE DOESN'T
HAPPEN.

BOXES CONTAIN MYSTERIES. BOXES **ARE** MYSTERIES.

UNTIL WE OPEN THEM, WE CAN NEVER REALLY BE SURE WHAT'S INSIDE.

I SHOULD BE INSIDE **THIS** BOX, AT **THIS** MOMENT. BUT I'M NOT.

I'M NOT.

00:04

OPERATING

SO WHERE AM I? **WHY** AM I?

WHAT'S INSIDE THE BOX?

DR. MANHATTAN

"LIGHTNING NEVER STRIKES THE SAME PLACE TWICE, REMEMBER?"

THE GILA FLATS INTRINSIC FIELD CHAMBER. ONE-FIFTEEN P.M., AUGUST 20, 1959.

THIS WAS WHERE I WAS REMADE.

THIS IS THE MOMENT I WAS REBORN.

HOW THEN CAN I BE STARING INTO AN EMPTY BOX?

HOW CAN THIS BE WHAT *IS*--

--IF *THIS* IS WHAT I REMEMBER?

IF *THIS* IS WHAT *HAPPENED*?

AS IT *MUST* HAVE HAPPENED--

--OR I WOULD NOT *BE* HERE TO *SEE* IT.

ONE-FIFTEEN P.M.

J. MICHAEL STRACZYNSKI script   ADAM HUGHES art

LAURA MARTIN colors   STEVE WANDS letters

ADAM HUGHES cover   P. CRAIG RUSSELL variant cover

CAMILLA ZHANG asst. editor   CHRIS CONROY assoc. editor   MARK CHIARELLO editor

WATCHMEN created by ALAN MOORE and DAVE GIBBONS

I WATCH MYSELF LEAVING, BUT I CANNOT BE LEAVING. BECAUSE I *DID* NOT LEAVE.

SOMETHING IS WRONG. SOMETHING IS--

EVERYTHING ALL RIGHT?

FINE. FOUND MY COAT JUST WHERE I LEFT IT. NOW I CAN GIVE JANEY BACK HER WATCH INSTEAD OF A HANDFUL OF MOLECULES--

--THAT'S STRANGE.

WHAT?

I FIXED IT THIS MORNING, BUT NOW IT'S NOT WORKING AGAIN. THE SECOND HAND ISN'T MOVING.

IT'S FROZEN AT ONE-FIFTEEN.

MAYBE YOU DIDN'T FIX IT AS GOOD AS YOU THOUGHT, DOC.

NO, YOU DON'T UNDERSTAND, WHEN I FIX A WATCH, IT *STAYS* FIXED.

NOT FROM MY PERSPECTIVE.

FIRST TIME FOR EVERYTHING, I GUESS.

AND I GUESS MAYBE IT WAS, BECAUSE IF HE HADN'T PASSED, YOU WOULDN'T HAVE BEEN HIRED TO REPLACE HIM, AND WE WOULD NEVER HAVE MET--

RIGHT ON TARGET! THE GENTLEMAN WINS A STUFFED BEAR FOR THE LITTLE LADY.

HERE YOU GO, MA'AM.

WHY, THANK YOU, I--

JUST A SECOND, THERE'S SOMETHING WRONG WITH THIS.

WHAT IS IT?

IT'S TORN BACK HERE. SEE?

OH, WELL, IT'S NOT IMPORTANT.

I DISAGREE. I THINK IT'S VERY IMPORTANT. SEE FOR YOURSELF.

JON--

YES, LOVE?

--WHAT'S IN THE BOX?

COULD BE *ANYTHING*. WHY DON'T YOU OPEN IT AND LOOK INSIDE?

I FIGURED I'VE GOT A FIFTY-FIFTY CHANCE OF HEARING WHAT I HOPE I HEAR, SO...

...YES OR NO?

YES! OH, DARLING, MOST DEFINITELY YES!

THANKS AGAIN FOR YOUR HELP!

MY PLEASURE, PAL. THAT'S MY SPECIALTY...THAT'S WHAT *I* DO.

PROVIDING THE ILLUSION OF FREE WILL.

WELL, NOW THAT I'M MOVING TO *D.C.* TO TEACH PHYSICS AT GEORGETOWN...

...WE BOTH KNOW THAT DREAM CAN *NEVER* COME TRUE, SO PUT IT OUT OF YOUR HEAD--

I WILL, I WILL.

COULD YOU TELL JANEY I'LL BE THERE IN TWO SHAKES?

YOU GOT IT.

MR. OSTERMAN...IS IT TRUE YOU'RE A SCIENTIST?

YES, IT IS.

IS IT HARD? I MEAN, THE MATH PART?

SOMETIMES. WHY?

WELL, I WANT TO BE A SCIENTIST TOO SOMEDAY, SO I CAN GO TO MARS.

AND WHY DO YOU WANT TO GO TO MARS?

SO I CAN SEE THE BLUE PEOPLE.

WHAT BLUE PEOPLE?

WELL, I DON'T THINK THERE ARE ANY BLUE MEN ON MARS, BUT WHO KNOWS, MAY SOMEDAY WE'LL GO THERE.

THIS BLUE MAN. HE AND HIS PEOPLE USED TO LIVE ON MARS BUT THEN THEY ALL DIED AND HE'S THE ONLY ONE LEFT.

JANEY? WHICH DRESSING ROOM ARE YOU IN?

GUESS!

ALWAYS A SURPRISE WITH YOU. OKAY--

--LEFT IT IS, THEN.

--RIGHT IT IS, THEN.

"LEFT..."

I OBJECT TO THIS IN THE **STRONGEST** POSSIBLE TERMS. THE PRESIDENT HAS NO RIGHT--

SOME DECISIONS ARE TOO IMPORTANT TO BE LEFT TO THE CONVENTIONAL MILITARY. THIS IS AN **INTELLIGENCE** ISSUE.

THEY'RE PUSSIES. YOU'RE **ALL** PUSSIES. SO LET'S GET THIS OVER WITH.

LET'S GET IT **ALL** OVER WITH.

"LEFT..."

"RIGHT..."

I OBJECT TO THIS IN THE **STRONGEST** POSSIBLE TERMS. THE PRESIDENT HAS NO RIGHT--

SOME DECISIONS ARE TOO IMPORTANT TO BE LEFT TO THE CONVENTIONAL MILITARY. THIS IS AN ISSUE OF **INTELLIGENCE**.

THEY DON'T WANT WAR ANY MORE THAN WE DO. SO LET'S TALK THIS OVER.

LET'S TALK IT **ALL** OVER.

‹CAPTAIN...A MESSAGE FROM THE AMERICANS. THEY SAY THEY WILL MOVE THEIR JUPITER MISSILES OUT OF TURKEY IF WE REMOVE OUR MISSILES FROM CUBA.›

"RIGHT..."

--THING I WANT TO DO IS TO EVEN *TRY* TO EXPLAIN THE SCHRODINGER'S CAT IDEA.

OH, COME--

WE BELIEVE IN YOU, WALLY, GIVE IT A SHOT.

WALLY! WALLY! WALLY! WALLY!

OKAY OKAYOKAY... JEEZ...

I'M SURE EITHER ONE OF THE GUYS AT THE TABLE WITH TWELVE-STORY BRAINS CAN EXPLAIN IT A LOT BETTER THAN ME, BUT...HERE'S HOW I UNDERSTAND IT.

"FIRST YOU MAKE A BOX AND YOU INSTALL A GLASS CAPSULE OF POISON GAS AND A MECHANISM WITH A 50/50 CHANCE OF BREAKING IT. SO IT COULD GO EITHER WAY.

"NEXT YOU PUT A CAT IN THE BOX. WHAT THE CAT THINKS ABOUT THIS IS ANYBODY'S GUESS.

"THEN YOU CLOSE THE BOX."

NOW, STANDING OUTSIDE THE BOX, ALL YOU KNOW IS THAT THERE'S A 50/50 CHANCE OF THE POISON BEING RELEASED.

SO THE CAT IN THE BOX IS EITHER ALIVE OR DEAD.

NO. ACCORDING TO QUANTUM PHYSICS, THE CAT IS BOTH ALIVE *AND* DEAD.

"IN QUANTUM PHYSICS, THE OBSERVER AFFECTS THE OBSERVED, THE WAY A PARTICLE IS A PARTICLE ONLY WHEN YOU'RE LOOKING AT IT. LOOK AWAY, IT BECOMES A WAVE. LOOK AT IT AGAIN, IT BECOMES A PARTICLE. SO THE CAT EXISTS IN BOTH STATES UNTIL THE QUANTUM OBSERVER OPENS THE BOX AND LOOKS INSIDE.

"THEN THE TWO QUANTUM POSSIBILITIES COLLAPSE INTO ONE REALITY.

"A LIVE CAT--

"--OR A DEAD CAT.

"POINT BEING, WHATEVER YOU MAY *THINK* YOU KNOW, YOU DON'T *REALLY* KNOW WHAT'S IN THE BOX UNTIL YOU OPEN IT UP AND LOOK INSIDE."

OF COURSE, THAT RAISES A QUESTION.

WHAT HAPPENS IF YOU DON'T OPEN THE BOX?

WELL, DEPENDING ON HOW YOU SET THE CONDITIONS OF THE EXPERIMENT, THE LONGER THE BOX REMAINS CLOSED...THE LONGER THE QUANTUM OBSERVER DOESN'T, WELL, *OBSERVE*...

...UNANTICIPATED FACTORS COULD BEGIN TO ALTER THE RESULTS--

"--MULTIPLYING THE EFFECTS, CREATING MORE RANDOM QUANTUM PROBABILITIES AND POCKET UNIVERSES, ALL OF THEM EQUALLY REAL, JOCKEYING WITH ONE ANOTHER FOR THE MOMENT WHEN THE BOX IS OPENED--"

--AND ALL THOSE POSSIBILITIES FINALLY COLLAPSE INTO ONE REALITY.

AS PERCEIVED BY THE QUANTUM OBSERVER.

IS THIS WHAT I AM? IS THIS WHAT I HAVE BECOME?

WHAT HAVE I DONE... WHAT HAVE I DONE?

"For I am become Death, the Destroyer of Worlds."

— Robert Oppenheimer, Director, The Manhattan Project

DR. MANHATTAN

DR. MANHATTAN

"I HAVE NAMED THE DISEASE. BUT WHAT IS THE CURE?"

EGO SUM

J. MICHAEL STRACZYNSKI script ADAM HUGHES art
LAURA MARTIN colors STEVE WANDS letters
ADAM HUGHES cover NEAL ADAMS variant cover
CAMILLA ZHANG asst. editor CHRIS CONROY assoc. editor MARK CHIARELLO editor
WATCHMEN created by ALAN MOORE and DAVE GIBBONS

BURRUP.

--THAT **THIS** WAS, INDEED, THE MOMENT.

1966.

IF CRIMEBUSTERS IS TO BECOME AN EFFICIENT CRIME FIGHTING ORGANIZATION, IT'S IMPORTANT THAT WE LEARN TO WORK TOGETHER.

DR. MANHATTAN "AN IMPERIALIST" FEIGN SAY

The New York Gazette

WHAT'S THE MATTER?

YOU WERE STARING AT THAT **GIRL** IS THE MATTER! NOW PAY **ATTENTION**.

I'D LIKE TO START BY PAIRING PEOPLE UP INTO GROUPS OF TWO, SO WE CAN LEARN ABOUT EACH OTHER'S IDEAS, GOALS, AND WHAT WE HOPE TO ACHIEVE WITH CRIMEBUSTERS. THAT'S WHY I HAD EACH OF YOU PUT YOUR I.D. ON A SLIP OF PAPER.

OUR FIRST IS DR. MANHATTAN, WHOSE PRESENCE HERE TONIGHT HONORS ALL OF US--

WHAT'S IN THE BOX?

IT WAS ALL A MATTER OF PERSPECTIVE.

--AND THE ONE HE'S PARTNERED WITH TONIGHT IS--

--IS--

AND PERSPECTIVES COULD BE CHANGED...WITH THE SLIGHTEST OF NUDGES.

--THE SILK SPECTRE.

Silk Spect

WHEN I CHANGED THE OUTCOME, I IMAGINED THAT I HAD SIMPLY CHANGED THE FUTURE, CREATING A NEW SET OF EVENTS AND POTENTIALITIES IN THE INSTANT BETWEEN WHAT *MIGHT* HAVE BEEN AND WHAT NOW *WAS*.

I ASSUMED THAT THE FUTURE *ME* THAT WOULD HAVE WORKED WITH RORSCHACH SIMPLY CEASED TO EXIST, OVERWRITTEN BY THE *ME* THAT WOULD WORK WITH LAURIE...THAT *LOVED* LAURIE.

IT NEVER OCCURRED TO ME THAT *BOTH* TIMELINES WOULD BECOME EQUALLY REAL, SPLINTERING REALITY IN BOTH DIRECTIONS, PAST AND FUTURE.

JON, I THINK I'D LIKE TO GO *HOME* NOW, PLEASE.

IN USING MY POWER TO BEND REALITY TO MY WILL, I ENSURED THAT MY CHOICES--

--MY *WILL*, WOULD BEGIN TO FORM *NEW* POCKET REALITIES WITH EVERY WHIM.

I HAVE NAMED THE DISEASE.

BUT WHAT IS THE CURE?

"WHAT YOU HAVE TO REMEMBER IS THAT THERE'S NOTHING BROKEN SO BAD THAT YOU CAN'T PUT IT BACK TOGETHER AGAIN WITH ENOUGH EFFORT."

SOMETIMES YOU CAN'T SEE WHAT THE PROBLEM IS UNTIL YOU GO *CLOSE*, UNTIL YOU LOOK DEEP *INSIDE*.

IT'S WHEN YOU LOOK BEYOND THE EDGE OF WHAT YOU *THINK* YOU KNOW--

--THAT YOU CAN FINALLY ARRIVE AT THE TRUTH.

HOW LONG DID IT TAKE BEFORE YOU WERE GOOD AT FIXING WATCHES?

IT TOOK A VERY LONG TIME, BUT I WAS DETERMINED TO LEARN...TO HONOR YOUR MOTHER'S SACRIFICE, HER--

...ACH...

HE LOOKS OFF. I KNOW THE REASON. I KNOW THE STORY. I LIVED IT WITH HIM.

IT WAS 1939. THE SECOND WORLD WAR HAD JUST BEGUN. I WAS TEN.

YOU SHOULD GO, JOSEF, WHILE YOU STILL HAVE TIME.

NO, I'M NOT LEAVING YOU. I CAN *PROTECT* YOU--

MY DARLING...YOU CAN'T CONTROL THE WORLD. SOONER OR LATER THEY WILL *FIND* ME AND THEY WILL *COME* FOR ME.

YOUR FRIENDS, YOUR COUSINS... THEY WERE NOT HAPPY WHEN YOU CHOSE TO MARRY A JEW. THEY HAVE NOTHING TO *GAIN* BY PROTECTING ME...AND MUCH TO *LOSE.* I AM TRAPPED HERE. THE SOLDIERS WILL NEVER LET ME THROUGH.

THE OTHERS WILL NOT TELL--

OF COURSE THEY WILL.

BUT YOU... YOU *CAN* ESCAPE. YOU CAN TAKE JON WITH YOU, GET TO THE PORT--

NO.

LISTEN TO ME. I CAN SELL WHAT'S LEFT OF MY MOTHER'S JEWELRY AND BUY A WAGON. WE CAN GO OUT BY BACK ROADS, TOO MUDDY FOR THEIR VEHICLES.

WE CAN SLIP AWAY IN THE MIDDLE OF THE NIGHT AND THEY WILL NEVER KNOW. I PROMISE WE CAN MAKE IT, INGE.

SAYING IT DOES NOT MAKE IT SO, JOSEF. YOU CANNOT MAKE THE WORLD WHAT YOU WANT BECAUSE YOU WANT IT.

BUT I LOVE YOU, AND I WILL GO WITH YOU--

"--EVEN INTO THE UNKNOWN."

JON...UP HERE.

YOU MUST HIDE HERE. IF WE ARE STOPPED, WE CAN SAY WE ARE BRINGING GOODS TO MARKET. IF THEY SEE YOU, THEY WILL KNOW WE ARE A FAMILY TRYING TO ESCAPE.

REMEMBER, YOU MUST NOT MAKE ANY NOISE, NO MATTER WHAT HAPPENS.

HYAH!

IN JUST FIVE KILOMETERS WE WOULD BE ABLE TO TURN ONTO THE BACK ROADS THAT LED TO THE BORDER.

"--NEVER FORGET THAT."

"...THERE'S NOTHING BROKEN SO BAD THAT YOU CAN'T PUT IT BACK TOGETHER AGAIN WITH ENOUGH EFFORT."

AS I LOOK AT THE RANDOM MOMENT THAT BROUGHT JANEY AND ME TOGETHER, I KNOW WHAT I MUST DO TO FIX THE DELICATE CLOCKWORK MECHANISM I HAVE BROKEN.

ONCE I BECAME THE QUANTUM OBSERVER, EVERY TIME I MADE A CHOICE IT FRACTURED REALITY, OVER AND OVER. SO THE ONLY WAY TO REUNITE THE TIMELINES IS BY ERASING ALL THOSE CHOICES.

THE IRONY IS NOT LOST ON ME.

I AM THE MOST POWERFUL BEING IN THE KNOWN UNIVERSE. I CAN DO ANYTHING.

BUT FOR THE WORLD TO BE WHAT IT NEEDS TO BE, WHAT IT MUST BE, I MUST SACRIFICE MY OWN CHOICES, MY OWN FREE WILL, SO THAT THEY CAN HAVE CHOICES.

IN THIS NEW, UNITED TIMELINE, WHATEVER I HAVE DONE IN THE FUTURE IS DONE, THE DECISIONS ARE MADE, AND CANNOT BE CHANGED. THEY ARE AS IRREVOCABLE AS THE CHOICES I MADE IN THE PAST.

BECAUSE ALL THOSE MOMENTS ARE THE SAME MOMENT, ONE MOMENT, ETERNAL AND SIMULTANEOUS.

LIKE MY MOTHER, I MUST GIVE UP ALL OF MY CHOICES SO THAT THEY CAN MAKE OF THIS REALITY WHAT THEY WISH.

EDITED REPLAY

SO I MUST FREEZE THAT ETERNAL MOMENT, FROZEN, LIKE THAT AMBER FLY.

BUT I MUST LET THIS UNIVERSE BECOME WHAT IT WILL NOW, INTERFERE NO MORE.

I AM LIMITLESS.

BEGIN MOVING FORWARD AND BACKWARD AT THE SAME TIME, ENSURING THAT EVERYTHING APPENED JUST THE WAY IT DID IN THE ORIGINAL TIMELINE, WITHOUT THE SLIGHTEST VARIATION.

OHH, YOU'RE THE NEW GUY. YOU'RE REPLACING HANK MEADOWS, RIGHT?

I AM?

I GUESS SO.

"HANK DIED LAST *FALL*--"

IN ONE TIMELINE, I CALL FROM PRINCETON ON THE ADVICE OF MY PROFESSORS TO GET SOME INFORMATION ON THE DECAY OF CERTAIN ATOMIC PARTICLES.

THE DISTRACTION ALLOWED HANK TO SEE THE UNCOVERED URANIUM CONTAINER BEHIND HIM IN TIME TO AVOID FATAL EXPOSURE...AND I AM NEVER OFFERED HIS JOB AT GILA FLATS.

SO I ENSURE THAT IN THIS TIMELINE, NO SUCH CALL COMES.

"--SOME *KINDA* TUMOR."

THERE'S HIS *PICTURE* BEHIND THE *BAR* THERE. THE GUY WITH *GLASSES*.

Y'KNOW, YOU'RE PRETTY *YOUNG* FOR A *RESEARCH* SCIENTIST.

"YEAH, WELL... MY *DAD* SORT OF *PUSHED* ME *INTO* IT."

IT'S AUGUST 7TH, 1945.

IN ONE TIMELINE, I ASK MY FATHER TO TAKE ME TO SEE THE BROOKLYN DODGERS. THE EXPERIENCE LEAVES HIM IN A GOOD MOOD, SO THAT WHEN HE LEARNS OF THE ATOMIC BOMB DROPPED ON HIROSHIMA, HIS REACTION IS TEMPERED.

SO I WIPE OUT THAT CHOICE, ENSURING THAT ON THIS HOT, HUMID BROOKLYN MORNING, WE ARE AT HOME, I WITH MY WATCHES, MY FATHER WITH HIS MEMORIES.

A SINGLE BOMB...ONE BOMB, AND THEY CAN WIN A WAR. SO WHAT WAS IT FOR, INGE? WHAT WAS ALL THAT DEATH FOR?

WHY DID I HAVE TO LOSE YOU?

JON? WHERE ARE YOU?

IN HERE. I'M PRACTICING ON YOUR OLD POCKET WATCH BEFORE IT'S TIME FOR SCHOOL.

FORGET POCKET WATCHES. HAVE YOU SEEN THE NEWS?

NEWS?

THEY DROPPED THE ATOMIC BOMB ON JAPAN! A WHOLE CITY, GONE.

ACH! THESE ARE NO TIMES FOR A REPAIRER OF WATCHES. THIS CHANGES EVERYTHING. THERE WILL BE MORE BOMBS. THEY ARE THE FUTURE.

"ATOMIC SCIENCE...THIS IS WHAT THE WORLD WILL NEED."

"MY DAD SORT OF PUSHED ME INTO IT--"

"WHAT'S IN THE BOX?"

"WHAT'S IN THE BOX?"

"WHAT'S IN THE BOX?"

"WHAT'S IN THE BOX?"

JANEY'S WATCH IS WORKING PERFECTLY.

TIME MOVES FORWARD AS IT SHOULD.

AND AS THE INFINITE NUMBER OF QUANTUM POSSIBILITIES COLLAPSE INTO ONE SINGULAR REALITY, IN THE INSTANT BEFORE THE ENERGY STRIKES--

--WE BECOME *AWARE* OF EACH OTHER. ALL OF US IN THE BOX TOGETHER.

PAST. PRESENT. FUTURE.

LIVE CAT.

DEAD CAT.

LIVE JON.

DEAD JON.

DR. MANHATTAN

"I HAVE A SMALL SUGGESTION REGARDING THE DESTRUCTION OF EARTH."

AT ONE-FIFTEEN P.M., AUGUST 20, 1959, I ENTERED THE INTRINSIC FIELD CHAMBER IN THE HOPE THAT I HAD PUT TIME, SPACE AND THE UNIVERSE ITSELF BACK TOGETHER AGAIN AS IT NEEDED TO BE. AS IT MUST BE.

"THOU KNOWEST, LORD, THE SECRETS OF OUR HEARTS; SHUT NOT THY MERCIFUL EARS TO OUR PRAYERS, BUT SPARE US, LORD MOST HOLY, O GOD MOST MIGHTY, O HOLY AND MERCIFUL SAVIOR--"

AND YET I'M AFRAID. AFRAID TO OPEN MY EYES. AFRAID THAT I DIDN'T GET IT RIGHT. AFRAID THAT I *MISSED* SOMETHING.

"--THOU MOST WORTHY JUDGE ETERNAL, SUFFER US NOT, AT OUR LAST HOUR, FOR ANY PAINS OF DEATH TO FALL FROM THEE. AMEN."

AMEN.

AMEN.

CHANGES IN PERSPECTIVE

J. MICHAEL STRACZYNSKI script   ADAM HUGHES art

LAURA MARTIN colors   STEVE WANDS letters

ADAM HUGHES cover   BILL SIENKIEWICZ variant cover

CAMILLA ZHANG asst. editor   CHRIS CONROY assoc. editor   MARK CHIARELLO editor

WATCHMEN created by ALAN MOORE and DAVE GIBBONS

I WATCH AS A BOX CONTAINING A MYSTERY IS LOWERED INTO THE SOIL.

AN *EMPTY* BOX. CONTAINING NOTHING. CONTAINING *ME.*

CONTAINING THE LAST REMNANTS OF ALL MY CHOICES.

JONATHAN OSTERMAN

MAY 5, 1929
AUGUST 30, 1959

DEAD. AND BURIED.

I'LL GIVE YOU CREDIT--

--WELL, SOME CREDIT--

--FOR HAVING DECIDED THAT IF YOU'RE GOING TO STEAL ANTIQUITIES--

--THE BRITISH MUSEUM WOULD BE THE PERFECT PLACE TO DO SO. ONE-STOP SHOPPING AS THEY SAY. A LITTLE CHINESE THIRD DYNASTY HERE--

--A LITTLE FIRST CENTURY ROME THERE. PRETTY SOON YOU'VE GOT A TIDY LITTLE COLLECTION ON YOUR HANDS. TOO BAD YOU FORGOT ONE THING.

YOU FORGOT TO CHECK THE PAPERS TO SEE IF I MIGHT BE VISITING.

THAT WAS *FAR* TOO *EASY.* ISN'T THERE *ANYONE* WHO CAN GIVE ME A REAL *CHALLENGE* THESE DAYS?

HELLO, ADRIAN.

YOU SHOULD'VE JOINED IN THE FUN.

THERE WAS NO POINT. YOU WERE WINNING. YOU HAD WON. YOU HAVE *ALWAYS* WON THIS FIGHT.

YOU'RE THE ONLY ONE I KNOW WHO ENGAGES NOT JUST IN DECLENSIONS OF *LANGUAGE* BUT OF *TIME* AS WELL.

THAT MAY SEEM A RATHER OBSCURE BIT OF JOLLITY, BUT TO AN AUDIENCE OF GRAMMARIANS OR PHYSICISTS, I'M A ROCK STAR.

SO WHAT CAN I DO FOR YOU?

WE NEED TO TALK, BUT NOT HERE. I REQUIRE PRIVACY.

ALL RIGHT, LET ME CALL MY CAR AND--

THIS WILL BE FASTER.

I TELL HIM ABOUT MY TRAVELS THROUGH SPACE AND TIME... ABOUT ACCIDENTALLY BECOMING A QUANTUM OBSERVER CAPABLE OF CREATING NEW UNIVERSES WITH EVEN THE MOST CASUAL ACT.

I TELL HIM ABOUT HOW MY DECISIONS DESTROYED THE EARTH, OVER AND OVER, EACH NEW COURSE COMING TO A FIERY END PUNCTUATED WITH MUSHROOM CLOUDS AS NUCLEAR WEAPONS OBLITERATED THE WORLD.

I TELL HIM ABOUT DESTROYING THE VERY ALTERNATE UNIVERSES I CREATED.

OTHER MEN HEARING SUCH THINGS WOULD FAINT, GO MAD OR RUN SCREAMING FROM THE ROOM.

HE ALLOWS ONLY A SMALL TIC IN HIS EXPRESSION, LASTING THE BAREST FLICKER OF A SECOND. NERVOUSNESS, I ASSUME.

FOR SOME REASON, I TAKE GREAT PLEASURE IN CATCHING IT.

"I MEAN THAT THE QUESTION, LIKE THE WORLD, DEATH, LIFE AND THE UNIVERSE ITSELF, ARE *ALL* MATTERS OF PERSPECTIVE."

ALL BOXES ARE
MYSTERIES,
CONTAINING
UNIVERSES.

JUST A LITTLE
ENERGY TO
ACCELERATE
EVOLUTION...
COMBINE PROTEINS
AND KNIT DNA INTO
SYMPHONIES OF
ELEGANCE AND
POTENTIALITY...

I CANNOT WAIT
TO SEE WHAT
THIS NEW BOX
REVEALS.

"WE ARE DOING GREAT THINGS HERE, EDGAR. AMAZING THINGS."

CHICAGO, 1937.

THE VAUDEVILLE CIRCUIT WAS PERFECT FOR A GUY ON THE MOVE. PERFORMERS ROTATED FROM TOWN TO TOWN EVERY MONTH, AND YOU GOT PAID IN CASH, NO QUESTIONS ASKED. *IF* YOU GOT PAID AT ALL.

La Reina del Vaudeville

SACHA MALDEN

VENUS GYPSY

I PICKED THE STAGE NAME **MOLOCH THE MYSTIC** BECAUSE I NEEDED SOMETHING ALLITERATIVE AND IT SOUNDED BETTER THAN **EDGAR THE ENTERTAINING.**

WHY MOLOCH? WHY NOT MASON OR MENTALLO OR MORRIS?

AT THE TIME I SAID IT WAS BECAUSE MOLOCH WAS AN AMMONITE **GOD** WORSHIPED BY THE PHOENICIANS AND THE CANAANITES, A BEING OF VAST SUPERNATURAL POWER.

WHICH WAS TECHNICALLY TRUE.

HE WAS ALSO THE GOD MOST ASSOCIATED WITH TH RITUAL SACRIFICE OF CHILDREN. AND SINCE IT WAS W JUST SUCH AN OFFERING THAT I STARTED MY CAREE EARNEST, WELL, IT JUST SEEMED APPROPRIATE.

NOBODY GOT THE REFERENCE. BUT THEN, WE WEREN'T PLAYING TO BIBLE SCHOLARS.

I PLAYED THREE SHOWS A DAY, BUT THE MONEY WAS BARELY ENOUGH TO PAY FOR WHATEVER ASSISTANT I ENDED UP WITH THAT WEEK, LET ALONE MEET MY NEEDS.

HEY EDDIE, CAN I GET MY MONEY NOW INSTEAD'A FRIDAY? I SAID I'D TAKE MY KID TO THE MOVIES.

GET OFF THE STAGE! WE WANT THE STRIPPERS!

SO I FOUN OTHER WAYS SUPPLEMENT MY INCOME

...FIND THE FACES, THE SECOND-STORY MEN,
THE MUSCLE AND THE GOONS-FOR-HIRE TO WORK
FOR ME WAS EASY. THEY WERE PRETTY GULLIBLE
WHEN IT CAME TO MAGIC. SOME OF THEM
ACTUALLY THOUGHT IT WAS THE REAL THING.

SO WHAT'S THE TARGET TONIGHT, BOSS?

WE ROBBED BANKS, HIJACKED TRUCKS,
KIDNAPPED PEOPLE...IT WAS LIKE THE
WHOLE WORLD WAS OUR CANDY STORE.

YOU WERE RIGHT, BOSS, ONE WORD FROM YOU AND BANG, DEAD ASLEEP.

OKAY, BOYS, LET'S START UNLOADING.

2 AB80

I INVESTED MONEY INTO WHAT WAS LEFT OF THE OPIUM
TRADE. THE DENS WERE GETTING RARE, BUT WERE
STILL USEFUL FOR INTRODUCING NEW WONDERS.
REEFER. COCAINE. HEROIN. UPPERS. DOWNERS.

I FOUND THERE WAS ALWAYS SOMETHING
TO BE GAINED FROM THOSE WHO NO LONGER
HAD ANY IDEA WHAT THEY WERE SAYING--

--I WANTED TO BRING THE DIAMONDS TO THE CUTTERS BUT MY FATHER SAID I'M NOT *SMART* ENOUGH OR *MATURE* ENOUGH SO WHEN THE PICKUP COMES MONDAY MORNING HE WANTS ME NOWHERE *NEAR* IT--

--AND THERE WERE *OTHER* BENEFITS
TO BEING THE ONE WHO HELD THE
KEYS TO THE KINGDOM OF DELIRIUM.

--JUST A LITTLE MORE, C'MON, I CAN MAKE YOU FEEL REAL GOOD, YOU *KNOW* I CAN, SO WHADDAYA SAY, JUST A LITTLE MORE--

FEW YEARS WE CONTINUED TO BATTLE IT OUT. BUT THE PROGRESSION WAS ALWAYS THE SAME.

...OPERATION.

...ABOUT IT.

THREE: IF THEY GOT THERE IN TIME, THEY ARRESTED ME AND SENT ME TO PRISON, FROM WHICH, SOONER OR LATER, I WOULD ESCAPE.

FOUR: IF THEY **DIDN'T** GET THERE IN TIME, SKIP STEP THREE.

AT LEAST FOR A WHILE.

BUT SOONER OR LATER THEY **WOULD** SHOW UP IN TIME, AND WE'D BE RIGHT BACK AT STEP THREE AGAIN.

I LEARNED TO LIE LOW FOR A FEW WEEKS BEFORE EACH PRISON BREAK, SO THEY WOULDN'T KNOW WHEN I'D MAKE MY MOVE.

WHILE I WAS IN WHATEVER PRISON THEY'D STUCK ME IN THAT TIME, I OFTEN FOUND MYSELF WANDERING OVER TO THE CHAPEL, ESPECIALLY WHEN I KNEW THEY WERE SLATED TO HOLD A CATHOLIC MASS.

WHY THAT ONE INSTE OF THE OTHERS? THE TIME I FIGURE WAS ABOUT THE RITU OR THE UNEXPECTE BEAUTY OF THE LA LITURGY, OR MAYBE

CHAPEL

--MAYBE EVEN--

NO.

I TURNED MY BACK. WALKED AWAY.

1378

EVERY TIME.

WHEN I BROKE BACK OUT ONTO THE STREETS AGAIN--A COMBINATION OF LOYA[L] THUGS AND THE MONEY I HAD STASHED AWAY IN SEVERAL OFFSHORE ACCOUNTS-- WENT RIGHT BACK TO THE WORLD I KNEW[.]

RUNNING HOUSE[S] OF PROSTITUTIO[N,] FETISH CLUBS[,] DRUG DENS.

ANYTHING THAT SERVED TO PROVE THAT THE SO-CALLED RESPECTABLE WORLD WAS EVERY BIT AS CORRUPT AS I WAS.

IT WAS A WORLD THAT ACCEPTED ME, THAT NEEDED ME, AND WHAT I COULD PROVIDE. A WORLD THAT ACTUALLY FOUND ME ATTRACTIVE--

--EVEN IF THAT WAS ONLY BECAUSE IT COULDN'T SEE STRAIGHT HALF THE TIME.

G'NNA BE NAUGHTY--

I WAS SO WRONG ABOUT YOU. YOU'RE BEAUTIFUL. YOU'RE TALENTED. AND THE THINGS I WANT TO DO TO YOU ARE--

G'NNA MAKE YOU FEEL REEEAL GOOD, MR. M.

--VERY, VERY NAUGHTY.

AND I HURT IT AGAIN--

--AND AGAIN--

--AND AGAIN--

--AND AGAIN AND AGAIN AND AGAIN AND AGAINAGAINAGAINAGAIN--

BUT EVERY NIGHT, AND EVERY MORNING, I WAS STILL ME.

STILL...ME.

WHERE DO YOU THINK YOU CAN GO THAT I CANNOT FOLLOW YOU?

WHERE I HAVE NOT **ALREADY** FOLLOWED YOU?

YOU ARE STANDING IN AN ALLEY.

YOU ARE SITTING IN A JAIL CELL.

IT'S ALREADY DONE.

SO HELP ME--

NO PARKING
YOU WILL BE TOWED

HELLO, EDGAR. I HEARD YOU WERE GETTING OUT TODAY.

I'VE BEEN GIVING YOU A LOT OF THOUGHT LATELY, AND THE UPSHOT IS, **EVERYBODY'S** ENTITLED TO A FRESH START.

SO I THOUGHT I'D SWING OVER, BUY YOU A HOT MEAL AND A CUP OF COFFEE--

--AND TALK ABOUT YOUR FUTURE.

--GOD.

FORGIVE ME, FATHER, FOR I HAVE SINNED

J. Michael Straczynski writer **Eduardo Risso** artist

Trish Mulvihill color Clem Robins letters Eduardo Risso cover artist
Matt & Brennan Wagner, Jim Lee & Alex Sinclair variant covers
Camilla Zhang assistant editor Mark Chiarello editor
Watchmen created by Alan Moore & Dave Gibbons

MOLOCH

"WE ALL MAKE MISTAKES, EDGAR."

THE ELEVEN-THIRTY
ABSOLUTION

J. Michael Straczynski writer
Eduardo Risso artist

Trish Mulvihill color Clem Robins letters Eduardo Risso cover artist
Olly Moss variant cover Camilla Zhang assistant editor Mark Chiarello edit
Watchmen created by Alan Moore & Dave Gibbons

WHERE MICHAEL JACKSON DAZZLED AUDIENCES WITH A NEW DANCE MOVE HE CALLS THE MOONWALK--

"YOU'RE DOING EXCELLENT WORK, EDGAR."

LET'S MAKE THIS ONE *REALLY* HARD TO FIND.

$+ \text{Ln}(x-3) - \text{Log2}(x+6)$

$+ \text{Ln}(x-3) - \text{Log2}(x+6)$

$+ \text{Ln}(x-3) - \text{Log2}(x-6)$

MARLA--

YES, MR. VEIDT?

--I'VE JUST SENT YOU THREE MORE FILES. PLEASE PRINT THEM UP AND HAVE THEM DROPPED OFF AT MR. JACOBI'S DESK.

OF COURSE.

DING DONG

JUST A MINUTE.

IT'S PRETTY HOT OUT THERE, WOULD YOU LIKE A *COKE* OR--

NO, I'M FINE, THANKS.

THESE THINGS ARE REAL *LIFE-SAVERS.*

YES...?

PACKAGE FOR YOU FROM MR. VEIDT.

OH, GOOD, I WAS GETTING WORRIED. PLEASE, COME IN.

CIGARETTES?

YES...AND NO. AFTER YOU-KNOW-WHO UP AND LEFT ME I STARTED IN ON THREE PACKS OF CIGARETTES A DAY. I WAS HURTING *MYSELF* BECAUSE I WAS MAD AT *HIM.*

DURING THE DAY I FEEL TIRED ALL THE TIME, AND AT NIGHT I CAN'T SLEEP.

MMM-HMM. ANY VOMITING, HEADACHES, LOOSE STOOLS?

ALL OF THE ABOVE. FOR **WEEKS** NOW.

COULD BE A LOW-GRADE INFECTION, OR THE FLU... GOT SOME REALLY NASTY VIRUSES RUNNING AROUND THESE DAYS.

I'M GOING TO PRESCRIBE SOME ANTIBIOTICS--

I'LL TRY TO HOLD THEM DOWN.

--AND SOME ANTI-NAUSEA MEDICATIONS. THIS WAY YOU WON'T LOSE ANY TIME AT WORK. YOU CAN PICK THEM UP AT THE FRONT DESK.

THANKS. GIVEN HOW MUCH DOCTOR VISITS COST, I REALLY APPRECIATE THAT MR. VEIDT HAS A CLINIC FOR HIS EMPLOYEES.

YES, HE'S A FINE MAN.

ICE JOB. ONE WOULD NEVER GUESS YOU HAD YOUR LICENSE REVOKED FOR--

WELL, NEVER MIND THAT. HOW IS HE?

DO WE HAVE WHAT WE NEED?

THE PROCESS IS CONTINUING. SLOW, BUT--

"BARRING A BIOPSY, WHICH WE'LL DO WHEN YOU GIVE THE OKAY, I'D SAY YES.

"WE HAVE IGNITION."

RAAFFFGGHH--

HUH-HUH...OGOD...

RRRAAGGH!

OH MAN...
BLOOD...

"WELL,
WE GOT
BACK THE
REPORTS
FROM THE
LAB."

THERE'S NO GOOD OR EASY WAY FOR ME TO SAY THIS, SO I'LL JUST SAY IT.

YOU HAVE STAGE THREE PROSTATE CANCER.

OGOD OGOD OGOD--

THE PROGNOSIS AT THIS STAGE ISN'T GOOD, BUT WE HAVE A WHOLE RANGE OF PROTOCOLS AND TREATMENTS NOW THAT--

BUT IT HAPPENED SO FAST! HOW DID I GET IT? WHY?

"--NO ONE REALLY KNOWS. SOME SAY IT CAN BE STRESS, GENETICS, EXPOSURE TO VARIOUS CHEMICALS--

"IT HAPPENS WHEN CELLS IN THE PROSTATE BECOME ABNORMAL, AND THE MUTATIONS IN THE CELLS' DNA MAKE THEM GROW AND DIVIDE FASTER THAN NORMAL CELLS, FORMING A TUMOR THAT INVADES THE REST OF THE BODY. AS TO WHY OR HOW--

"--OR RADIATION, THOUGH I THINK WE CAN SAFELY RULE THAT OUT IN YOUR CASE.

"FOR WHAT IT'S WORTH, HOWEVER, I'VE SPOKEN TO MR. VEIDT AND HE HAS PLEDGED TO DO EVERYTHING HE CAN TO HELP YOU.

"HE SAYS YOU'RE VERY, **VERY** IMPORTANT TO HIM."

AAAAAAAAA!

OH GOD, PLEASE...

PLEASE, THIS MUST BE A **MISTAKE**. YOU HAVE THE **WRONG PERSON**.

GOOD THING I DECIDED TO STAY ON THE JOB ANOTHER DAY, MR. VEIDT.

LOOKS LIKE YOUR TARGET JUST HAD ANOTHER VISITOR. AND YOU'LL NEVER GUESS WHO.

"NO ONE CAN GUESS HOW LONG DR. MANHATTAN WILL REMAIN IN HIDING ON THE PLANET MARS."

THE MAN DESCRIBED AS THE MOST POWERFUL FORCE IN THE UNIVERSE WAS LAST SEEN ERUPTING IN A RAGE DURING A TALK SHOW ON **ABC.**

FOR THOSE WHO MISSED IT, HERE'S ANOTHER LOOK.

I WONDER IF YOU REMEMBER **WALLY WEAVER.** BACK IN THE EARLY SIXTIES THE NEWSPAPERS CALLED HIM **DR. MANHATTAN'S BUDDY.**

HE DIED OF **CANCER** IN 1971.

I BELIEVE IT WAS **SUDDEN** AND QUITE **PAINFUL.**

I REMEMBER WALLY AS A GOOD FRIEND. I ATTENDED HIS **FUNERAL.**

HOW ABOUT **EDWARD W. JACOBI,** ALSO KNOWN AS **MOLOCH?** YOU ENCOUNTERED **HIM SEVERAL** TIMES DURING THE SIXTIES IN **BATTLES, CONFLICTS,** WHATEVER IT IS YOU SUPER-PEOPLE **DO.**

DID YOU KNOW THAT JACOBI **ALSO** HAS TERMINAL CANCER?

BUT... HOW DID THEY FIND OUT, NO ONE'S SUPPOSED TO--

THEN HOW ABOUT **THIS** ONE.

DID YOU KNOW THAT MISS **JANEY SLATER,** LINKED ROMANTICALLY WITH YOU IN THE SIXTIES IS CURRENTLY SUFFERING FROM LUNG CANCER?

"DOCTORS HAVE GIVEN HER SIX MONTHS TO LIVE."

BUT SHE SAID SHE HAD A CLEAN BILL OF HEALTH, SHE--

THE CIGARETTES... OH GOD...OH GOD, NO--

NOTICE ANY **CONNECTION?**

BECAUSE FROM WHERE **I'M** STANDING, IT'S STARTING TO LOOK PRETTY **CONCLUSIVE.**

HELLO, EDGAR.

DON'T BE AFRAID. I'M HERE TO TELL YOU WHAT THIS IS ALL ABOUT.

I'M HERE TO TELL YOU THE TRUTH.

SO HELP ME GOD.

--AND USING DR. MANHATTAN'S TELEPORTATION ENERGIES TO CREATE A FALSE FLAG ATTACK WILL UNITE THE PLANET.

IT WILL MEAN AN END TO WAR.

AN END TO FIGHTING.

IT WILL TAKE US FROM THE BRINK OF TOTAL NUCLEAR ANNIHILATION TO A NEW ERA OF PEACE.

WE WILL CHANGE THE FUTURE, EDGAR, JUST AS I PROMISED WE WOULD.

IT'S POSSIBLE THAT YOU COULD MANAGE TO THROW MY PLANS OUT OF GEAR BY GOING TO THE POLICE, OR THE OTHER COSTUMES. I COULD HAVE JUST KILLED YOU WHEN I WALKED IN HERE.

BUT I WANTED TO GIVE YOU A CHOICE.

EXCEPT PERHAPS FOR THE EGYPTIAN GODS OF OLD, I'VE NEVER BELIEVED IN ANY GOD OTHER THAN MYSELF. I COULD NEVER WRAP MY BRAIN AROUND THE IDEA OF "CHRIST DIED FOR OUR SINS...CHRIST DIED TO SAVE THE WORLD."

UNTIL TONIGHT.

UNTIL YOU.

YOU'RE DYING, EDGAR. WE BOTH KNOW THAT. SOONER OR LATER, WE ALL DIE. BUT WHAT'S UNSPEAKABLY RARE IS THE CHANCE FOR ONE'S DEATH TO SERVE A GREATER *PURPOSE.*

YOU WANTED TO ATONE...AND AS IT SAYS IN THE BIBLE, "AN EYE FOR AN EYE." A LIFE FOR A LIFE. MANY DIED AT YOUR HANDS, EDGAR. YOUR DEATH *IS* YOUR ATONEMENT.

BUT IT CAN BE MORE THAN THAT... *MUCH* MORE.

YOU BELIEVE THAT CHRIST DIED TO SAVE THE WORLD. YOU HAVE THAT POWER, RIGHT HERE, RIGHT NOW.

DO YOU BELIEVE THAT MY STRATEGY WILL WORK?

YES...YES, I DO. IT *WILL SAVE* THE WORLD. IT'S TERRIBLE...IT'S BEAUTIFUL...IT *WILL* WORK...AND--

BEFORE WATCHMEN: NITE OWL #1 VARIANT COVER
Art by JIM LEE with SCOTT WILLIAMS & ALEX SINCLAIR

NITE OWL

BEFORE WATCHMEN: NITE OWL #1 VARIANT COVER
Art by KEVIN NOWLAN

BEFORE WATCHMEN: NITE OWL #2 VARIANT COVER
Art by DAVID FINCH with SONIA OBACK

NITE OWL

BEFORE WATCHMEN: NITE OWL #3 VARIANT COVER
Art by CHRIS SAMNEE with MATT WILSON

BEFORE WATCHMEN: NITE OWL #4 VARIANT COVER
Art by ART BY ETHAN VAN SCIVER with HI-FI COLOUR DESIGN

DR. MANHATTAN

BEFORE WATCHMEN: DR. MANHATTAN #1 VARIANT COVER
Art by JIM LEE with SCOTT WILLIAMS & ALEX SINCLAIR

BEFORE WATCHMEN: DR. MANHATTAN #1 VARIANT COVER
Art by PAUL POPE with LOVERN KINDZIERSKI

DR. MANHATTAN

BEFORE WATCHMEN: DR. MANHATTAN #2 VARIANT COVER
Art by P. CRAIG RUSSELL

BEFORE WATCHMEN: DR. MANHATTAN #3 VARIANT COVER
Art by NEAL ADAMS

DR. MANHATTAN

BEFORE WATCHMEN: DR. MANHATTAN #4 VARIANT COVER
Art by BILL SIENKIEWICZ

MOLOCH

BEFORE WATCHMEN: MOLOCH #1 VARIANT COVER
Art by MATT WAGNER with BRENNAN WAGNER

MOLOCH

BEFORE WATCHMEN: MOLOCH #1 VARIANT COVER
Art by JIM LEE with SCOTT WILLIAMS & ALEX SINCLAIR

PRESENTING

MOLOCH
MYSTIC

BEFORE WATCHMEN: MOLOCH #2 VARIANT COVER
Art by OLLY MOSS

DAZZLING FINAL PERFORMAN

Nite Owl character study by ANDY KUBERT and JOE KUBERT with BRAD ANDERSON

Before Watchmen: NIte Owl cover sketches for issues 1, 2 and 4 by ANDY KUBERT

Cover progression for Before Watchmen: Dr. Manhattan #4 by ADAM HUGHES

Various warm-up sketches and pen test for Before Watchmen: Dr. Manhattan by ADAM HUGHES

**Cover sketches for Before Watchmen: Dr. Manhattan #1 with
layout and final for Before Watchmen: Dr. Manhattan #1, page 2 by ADAM HUGHES**

BIOGRAPHIES

J. MICHAEL STRACZYNSKI is an award-winning writer for film, television and comics. A former journalist for *The Los Angeles Times* and Time Inc., he has worked on such series as *The Twilight Zone* and *Murder She Wrote* and created *Jeremiah, Crusade* and *Babylon 5*, for which he may be best known. He penned the screenplay for Clint Eastwood's *Changeling*, for which he received a British Academy Award nomination, and *Ninja Assassin* for the Wachowskis. His work has earned him two Hugo Awards as well as the Saturn, the Eisner, the Inkpot and the Ray Bradbury Award, among many others. His comics work includes *Rising Stars* and *Midnight Nation* for Top Cow/Image, *The Amazing Spider-Man, Supreme Power,* and *Thor* for Marvel, and SUPERMAN and WONDER WOMAN for DC Comics.

ANDY KUBERT began his career at DC Comics illustrating the first highly successful BATMAN VERSUS PREDATOR and ADAM STRANGE series. Andy went on to Marvel Comics' popular *X-Men* title, which was consistently a sales juggernaut and remained their top-selling comic during his six-year run. At Marvel he also illustrated such titles as *Ghost Rider, Captain America, Ultimate X-Men* and the *Marvel 1602* miniseries in which he collaborated with *New York Times* best-selling author Neil Gaiman and which earned a 2005 Quill Award for Best Graphic Novel. He has worked on BATMAN with Grant Morrison and FLASHPOINT with Geoff Johns, and on BEFORE WATCHMEN: NITE OWL with Joe Kubert and J. Michael Straczynski.

In addition to having been named to *Wizard* magazine's Top Ten Artists, Andy is also an instructor at the Joe Kubert School of Cartoon and Graphic Art in Dover, New Jersey.

Born in 1926, **JOE KUBERT** began his comics career at the age of eleven as an apprentice in Harry "A" Chesler's comic book production house. He has worked in the industry ever since, and in his more than seventy years in the field he has produced countless memorable stories for countless characters, including DC's Hawkman, Tarzan, Enemy Ace, Batman and the Flash. Kubert also edited, wrote and illustrated the DC title SGT. ROCK, which, beginning under its original title OUR ARMY AT WAR, he contributed to for thirty years.

Kubert was also one of the first creators to embrace the long-form version of comics that became known as graphic novels, with his first two works in this medium being a graphic novel of his best-known creation, the heroic caveman Tor, and the war adventure Abraham Stone. Kubert has also been a pioneer in the realm of comics education. In 1976 he founded the first and only accredited school devoted solely to the art of cartoon graphics: The Joe Kubert School of Cartoon and Graphic Art in Dover, New Jersey, which has since produced many of today's leading cartoonists.

BILL SIENKIEWICZ (pronounced sin-KEV-itch) is an Eisner-winning, Emmy-nominated artist best known for revamping the style of comic and graphic novel illustration from 1980 onward, most notably with Marvel Comics' *Elektra: Assassin* and his acclaimed graphic novel *Stray Toasters*, earning him an international reputation and cult status across media industries.

ADAM HUGHES began working in comics at the age of 19, in 1985. In 1988 Adam lent his talents to a comic book called MAZE AGENCY, a book that many consider to be his first real artistic "run" on a title. He did over a year on the book, of both interior and cover artwork. In 1989 Adam began working on his first "mainstream" comic book title: DC Comics' JUSTICE LEAGUE. He worked on the book for almost two years, doing covers and interiors until 1990, and then switching to supplying artwork for just the covers. Eight years later, Adam began what many see as his most acclaimed cover work. Adam's recognizably strong and elegantly drawn women have graced the covers of four years' worth of DC Comics' WONDER WOMAN.

Today Adam is best known as a cover artist. He pencils, inks and colors his own covers, using both traditional and digital mediums. His artwork can be seen on an amazing assortment of comic book covers as well as many places outside the comic book industry.

A native of Leones, Argentina, **EDUARDO RISSO** began drawing professionally in 1981 with the magazine strips "Julio Cesar" and "El Angel." In 1986 he began an association with writer Carlos Trillo that continues to this day — their collaborations include the titles *Fulù, Simon: An American Tale, J.C. Benedict, Chicanos* and *Borderline*. After breaking into American comics in 1997, Risso first worked with writer Brian Azzarello on the 1998 Vertigo miniseries JONNY DOUBLE, which led directly to their partnership on 100 BULLETS as well as the DC graphic novel BATMAN: BROKEN CITY. Risso's work on 100 BULLETS has earned him three Eisner Awards, two Harvey Awards and the Yellow Kid Award.